Becoming a Successful Graphic Designer

Neil Leonard

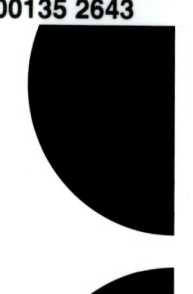

creative careers

Fairchild Books
An imprint of Bloomsbury Publishing Plc

B L O O M S B U R Y
LONDON · OXFORD · NEW YORK · NEW DELHI · SYDNEY

Fairchild Books
An imprint of Bloomsbury Publishing Plc

Imprint previously known as AVA Publishing

50 Bedford Square   1385 Broadway
London   New York
WC1B 3DP   NY 10018
UK   USA

www.bloomsbury.com

FAIRCHILD BOOKS, BLOOMSBURY and the Diana logo are trademarks of Bloomsbury Publishing Plc

British Library Cataloguing–in–Publication Data

A catalogue record for this book is available from the British Library.

ISBN: PB: 978-1-4725-9119-7

ePDF: 978-1-4725-9120-3

Library of Congress Cataloging–in–Publication Data

Leonard, Neil (Graphic designer)

Becoming a successful graphic designer / Neil Leonard. -- [First Edition].

pages cm

Includes bibliographical references and index.

ISBN 978-1-4725-9119-7 (pbk. : alk. paper) -- ISBN 978-1-4725-9120-3 (epdf) 1. Commercial art--Vocational guidance. 2. Graphic arts--Vocational guidance. I. Title.

NC1001.L46 2015

741.6023--dc23

2014049031

Series: Creative Careers

Typeset by Neil Leonard

Printed and bound in China

0.1

Ночью

At Night

0.1
Unloud: an artist book developed for
British artist Duncan Higgins.
Studio: du.st
Website: www.du.st
Client: Duncan Higgins

Becoming a successful graphic designer

Having studied for a qualification in graphic design, visual communication, or perhaps even illustration, you will naturally be thinking about taking your first steps into the world of work, and becoming a "graphic designer". But what makes a "successful graphic designer"?

Many would argue that studying a subject such as graphic design for a number of years and then going on to work in a related discipline is success in itself. Working in an environment that is linked to your passion, alongside others who feel the same way about their job is success.

When it comes to graphic design, success can be measured in very specific ways: the transition from junior to senior designer for example, or winning a big pitch. You may wish to grow your own agency, or work for a well–known firm with a great reputation and an office in a capital city. Simply learning new skills, or overcoming challenges related to a particularly difficult design problem, will offer measures of accomplishment, and through this, success.

Every person in the design industry you speak to will have different advice and insight, and they will want to share the "secrets to their success" but your journey will never be the same as theirs, so take from their advice broad ideas and don't try to follow the exact steps. This book contains advice and insight from designers working at all levels of the industry, so apply their learning to your circumstances and read what they have to say, then make it your own.

Success is a very individual thing and you are the only person who can define whether or not you are successful. You set the benchmark, and you will know when this has been met. Some successes will be measured with a degree of retrospect, but sometimes in the moment when you've created a piece of work that you are particularly proud of and its been signed off by the client, you will know you are successful.

Of all of the creative arts, graphic design can be the most exciting and challenging environment to work in, and when a designer is at the top of their game, it is hugely rewarding.

Graphic Design is a diverse and creative area; it sits at the cross section between the creative industries and the commercial sphere, and it incorporates aspects of many other disciplines.

Since the term "graphic design" was coined in the 1920s (a development from the term "graphic arts") the discipline has developed constantly. Initially a graphic designer was a trade's person that worked with paper, text and images — this developed quickly to incorporate branding, marketing and advertising. Now a graphic designer will work on animation, print and web projects in a single day.

0.2 + 0.3

Art Direction & Design Aizone, a luxury department store in the Middle East. Taking the vibrant nature of the brand and presenting it in campaigns that are printed in newspapers, magazines, and billboards throughout Lebanon.

Studio: Sagmeister & Walsh

Website: www.sagmeisterwalsh.com

Client: Aizone

While it is hard to pin down exactly what a career in graphic design entails as the industry changes so often, there are some constants and fortunately the real thrill of the job is often found in the discovery of the new. While you may work across a variety of media the idea and attention to detail are still the most important thing, and no graphic design project will succeed if it is not thoroughly considered. This focus on ideas above technique ensures that there is a constant focus on the "new" and the right contemporary tools for the job are learnt and deployed.

In addition to the various tools of the trade, there are a variety of roles that can be explored. You don't always have to go the traditional route of work experience/internships to junior designer roles. Now the necessary tools for the trade are affordable and more commonplace there is nothing to stop you setting up yourself. *Becoming a Successful Graphic Designer* will offer you insight into the skills, abilities and practical steps needed to work for yourself, set up on your own, or work in shared co–working spaces.

Previously many of the jobs a designer will undertake while working on a project would be split between many people; technology now means that a single person can achieve the work of many. Throughout the history of print we had designers (creators of the layout) and typesetters (those that physically put the layout together). Additionally, the division between those that work in areas such as advertising, marketing and print has largely eroded: as projects will incorporate all of these areas so it makes sense for the same designer or team to work across them. Some areas are still very specific as they involve such specialist knowledge or skills that it is not always possible to work broadly; coding and copywriting are two examples of this.

Technology plays a great part in shaping the current landscape of the industry, but social changes can have equal impact. As a designer it is up to you to understand the way people interact with your content and understand what motivates them to buy a certain product, or vote for a particular political party.

Becoming a Successful Graphic Designer provides you with the knowledge necessary to work in this vibrant and constantly evolving area. Within these pages you will gain the essential insight needed to help you decide whether you want to work in an established design firm, set up your own, or develop a freelance career. We have the best advice gathered from people across the industry, both established and emerging faces, all of whom have worked across this industry and are experts in their field.

This title is part of the Creative Careers series from Fairchild Books, designed to help bridge the gap between academia and a first job in the creative industries. Brimming with helpful tips and facts about the world of work, they offer an essential guide for any emerging creative practitioner.

BIC

PRO MIS E

1.1 + 1.2

The Advertising and Design Club of Canada needed to drive membership. Not only did Blok Design work to add greater, more robust benefits for its members, they also created this provocative piece designed to communicate the advantages and prestige of belonging to such an august community of like—minded thinkers and creators.

Studio: Blok Design

Website: www.blokdesign.com

Clients: The Advertising and Design Club of Canada

BIC

CHAPTER 1
GRAPHIC DESIGN ENTERPRISE

Where do graphic designers work? What do they do on a day–to–day basis? Who do they work with, and how do they find clients and jobs? Perhaps most importantly, you might be asking, where can I fit in and how do I get there?

This chapter will demystify the world of graphic design and cover many of the basics you will need to know before embarking on a long and fruitful career in the industry.

1.2

In this chapter we will:

- *Outline traditional definitions of "graphic design" and look at how these have changed to encompass a much broader range of disciplines.*

- *Establish who works in graphic design and where. Identify the skills and attributes that will help you to succeed as a graphic designer.*

- *Suggest ways to stay career–focused and up–to–date with the latest developments in graphic design.*

Understanding graphic design

As you've picked up this book you will likely have some idea as to the nature of the subject of graphic design, and what being a graphic designer involves. However, the expectations and needs of the client and the designer are forever changing, and so are the requirements of the job.

Traditional definitions of graphic design focus on the discipline's close relationship with text and imagery, the context in which the work is displayed (print, web, advertising, etc.), and the intention to communicate a message to a desired audience. However, graphic design as an industry is in a constant state of flux and this definition widens with every technical innovation, or new idea. While many concern themselves with boundaries, the most successful graphic designers look past these and are not concerned whether the outcome is digital or print; their only concern is whether they have fulfilled the brief in the most clever, innovative and original way.

So, is graphic design about ideas? Or is it about skills? Is it a mindset? Is it all about problem solving?

The short answer to the questions above is yes; it's about all of these things and a great deal more.

You may look at the discipline as a sector within the creative arts, or, conversely, you may view if from a commerce standpoint. The focus of your work as a graphic designer might vary from innovative charity campaigns, to cutting–edge digital innovations, and the skills required of a graphic designer today range from traditional letterpress techniques to emerging, innovative technologies. You will need to be prepared for all of this, and many other requirements, some of which aren't event invented as yet.

Ultimately a career in graphic design is what you make it, and as someone entering the industry, you have the power to make choices that you feel are right and shape your future. You can choose the type of work you wish to do, the companies you work for, and the clients you work with. All work has a focus and you can choose where you place yours, be it for global commerce leaders looking to access the greatest audience possible, or for startups and small charities that are just looking to get a foot on the ladder.

"You have no idea what people actually do, day to day, in their jobs. Before deciding that one career or another suits you, actually find out what people on that path do."

Kevin Hassall, Our Man in Belgrade

1.3

1.4

1.5

1.3 — 1.5

A promotional campaign for the Railroad Museum of Asturias. Here the designer used simple geometric shapes to create a dynamic, playful and evocative image.

Studio: Atipo

Website: www.atipo.es

Client: Railroad Museum of Asturias

1.6 — 1.8

Bariol type catalog.

Studio: Atipo

Website: www.atipo.es

Client: Atipo

1.6

1.7

1.8

Where do graphic designers work?

Graphic design is a relatively new term that is used as a catchall for several associated sectors, as well as being an industry in itself. To gain the knowledge and skills to work in publishing, advertising, web design, motion graphics, typographic design, and many other similar professions, a person will likely study graphic design.

While many of graphic design's founding principles can be tracked back to trades such as sign writing, printing and typesetting, the subject itself is a rich meeting point of several disciplines, backed up by a clear investigative thought process. The ideas that inform the discipline can be traced to politics, sociology, finance, philosophy, psychology and many other associated areas of thought, and these have made it a visually rich and intellectually vibrant sector to work in.

Training as a graphic designer, you should develop necessary knowledge of messaging, legibility, readability, scale and proportion, semiotics, making,

developing concepts and delivering to the requirements of a brief. These broad skills are required in all of the aforementioned areas, along with an extra slice of specialism that is largely concerned with the nature of the deliverable: is it printed, digital, or a campaign that ranges across several outcomes?

Beyond the particular deliverable emphasis, the clients you will work with range from public sector bodies to the commercial sector, small–scale startups to charities and not–for–profits. You may specialize and concentrate on working with one type of client, or you may work broadly. Still, with any one client, regardless of size and sector, you may touch on projects as varied as branding, packaging, moving image, design in the environment, exhibitions design, and much more.

Working with large (possibly multinational) commercial companies will normally yield the greatest financial returns and afford you the most exposure.

Working with charities and not–for–profits can be exciting, and this may be your most creative work, but it normally comes with a finite budget. However, as they tend to have little money to spend on advertising and design these clients are often open to taking risks in order to reach the larger audience.

Beyond this there are many roles that roll across the full range of disciplines associated with graphic design. While the most obvious destination for many studying the subject is to work as a designer, there are all sorts of roles that are client side and business side, from account management to studio management.

"Curiosity is key. Listen, absorb, and constantly connect dots. Go to galleries, watch films, travel, walk home a different route. Do interesting things, and interesting things will happen to you and your work.

Leave room for accidents. Accidents are blessings in disguise and most of the time turns your alright ideas into never before seen great ideas."

Adpreneurs

1.9

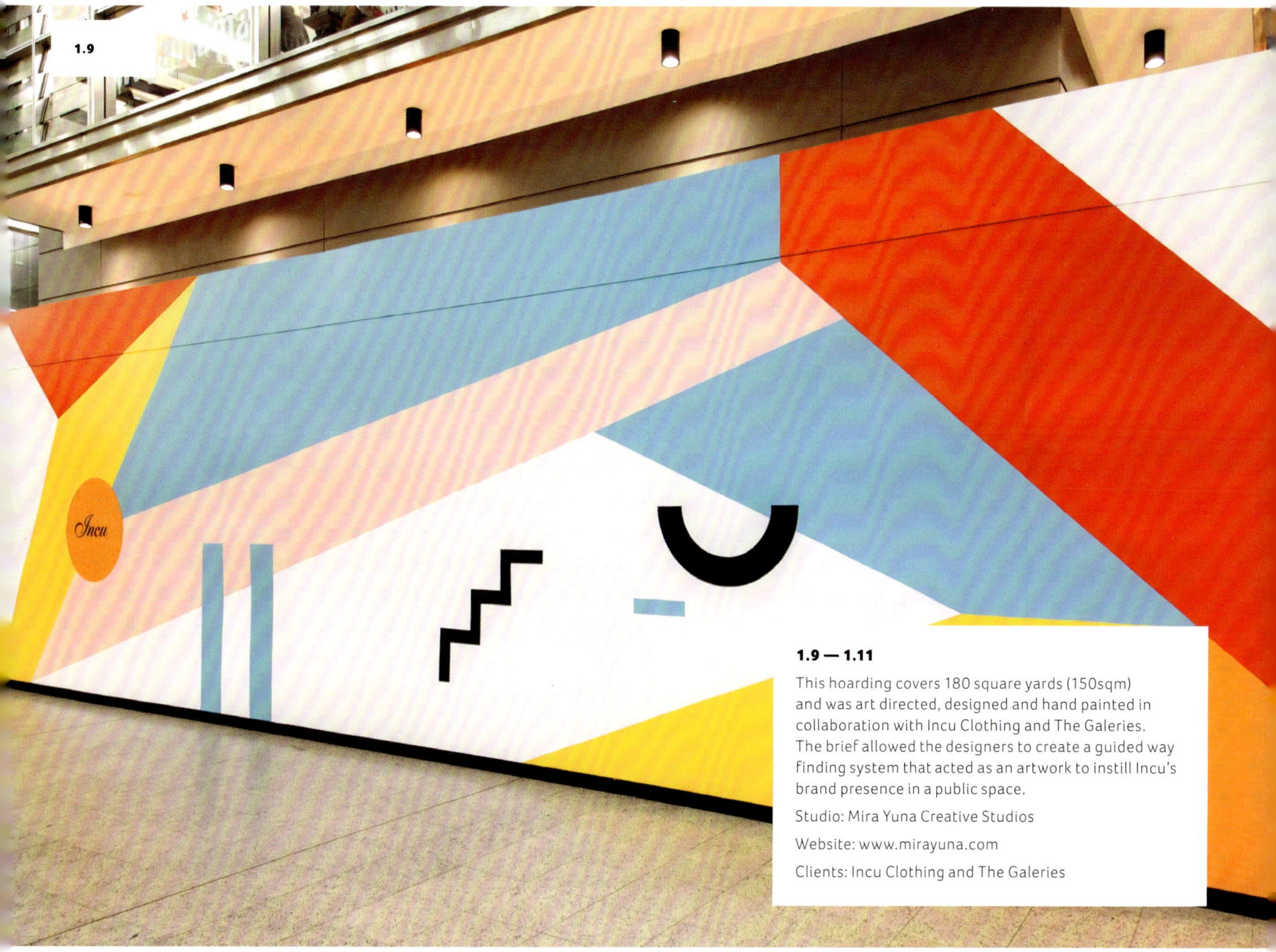

1.9 — 1.11

This hoarding covers 180 square yards (150sqm) and was art directed, designed and hand painted in collaboration with Incu Clothing and The Galeries. The brief allowed the designers to create a guided way finding system that acted as an artwork to instill Incu's brand presence in a public space.

Studio: Mira Yuna Creative Studios

Website: www.mirayuna.com

Clients: Incu Clothing and The Galeries

1.10

1.11

The essential skills

To survive in design you need to have the right mix of attributes. Unfortunately, everyone you ask will have their own definition of what the right mix is and no two employers or clients will agree on every aspect. However, there are some skills that no designer should be without. We'll begin by discussing these here — and by cultivating and developing these skills, you'll be one step closer to getting hired and enjoying a long and fruitful career in graphic design.

Problem solving

Graphic design is all about problem solving. This does not mean that every brief will be a problem, or that it will even be phrased that way, but the creative and critical analytical mindset that is applied to problem solving can be utilized through all graphic design projects.

Imagine getting locked outside of your house. You will likely run through a number of scenarios and quickly determine their pros and cons. You might call a neighbor or friend who has a spare set of keys (forward planning), but at the same time you don't want to inconvenience them (a project/time management issue). A locksmith could help, but they cost money (a cost/benefit analysis) and if you don't have the funds (or budget) to pay, then this course of action is impossible. You could break a window, but this might result in your neighbors calling the police (bad publicity) and they might arrest you if you have no ID (a moral issue or perhaps an ethical one). If you are feeling especially enterprising, you might find other ways into the house such as picking a lock, or finding an open window, but if you want to play it safe you might simply wait for a co–habitant to arrive home.

In just the same way, when you are faced with a design task, your mind will jump between a range of different approaches to solving it, and you should be able to quickly evaluate appropriateness, affordability, impact and other criteria.

Design theory

The day–to–day work of a practicing designer may be largely hands–on in terms of working in the various stages of the design process, but taking time out to engage with design theory is essential for two reasons: fresh ideas and fresh thinking. Engaging with design theory does not necessarily mean reading textbooks written by long–dead practitioners, although understanding the thought processes of others can be a source of inspiration. The very casual act of flicking through a book about design or painting or typography, or a consumer magazine can help you generate ideas for a design problem and think through design decisions in addition to understanding why you are making them. Reading and exposing yourself to the collective wisdom of art and design practice will help you critically analyze what you do on a day–to–day basis and pre–empt problems.

Theory is an ever present factor in design, whether it is color theory that determines how images are printed or displayed on screen, thus presenting technical opportunities and challenges, or Gestalt laws of perceptual organization that can help you order and place the very basic building blocks of your design. The point is that there is a large body of design theory available that can help you arrive at workable design solutions so that you do not have to reinvent the wheel with every project. Continuing to read and apply design theory can result in your developing a particular specialization that may make you more marketable as a designer, for example, magazine layouts, posters or book design.

1.13

1.12 + 1.13

ITI Computers is an established software company that focuses on the development of complex business solutions for the tourism industry. Bunch was asked to redesign the identity for Diventa, their most successful product. This was then applied to stationery, folders and a range of other promotional materials, including a brochure for Diventa that features three different covers.

Studio: Bunch Design

Website: www.bunchdesign.com

Clients: ITI Computers

1.14

1.14 — 1.17

Motherbird was asked to create a campaign to launch Billy Blue College of Design's new Melbourne Campus.

Paper models were constructed, photographed and retouched, resulting in a series of images that blur the line between tangible and intangible, tactile and digital.

Studio: Motherbird

Website: www.motherbird.com.au

Clients: Billy Blue College of Design

BILLY BLUE COLLEGE OF DESIGN®

ADVENTURE INTO DESIGN
THINKING | MAKING | CONNECTING

MELBOURNE, SYDNEY, BRISBANE
Join us at www.billyblue.edu.au or call 1300 851 245 to find out more

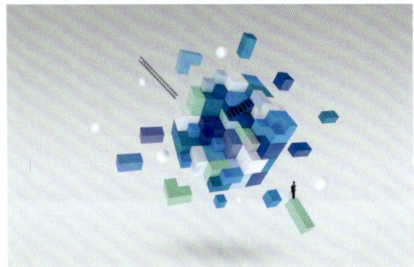

1.15

1.16

1.17

Communication skills

No matter what role you take on in a design studio, good communication skills are absolutely essential. A large part of everyone's day is taken up with communicating with other people, and the smoother this goes, the more design work gets done. Good communication with a client and within a design team is essential to ensure that a brief is sufficient to achieve the desired results. Being communicative will make you an easy person to work with. Clients and employers tend not to like working with people who are difficult to manage or uncooperative!

Good communication requires honesty and integrity as at times you will be working with confidential information and sensitive data, both from the client and your employers, and this has to be respected. Many projects require that nondisclosure agreements are signed and a breach of confidentiality can cost the agency both money and clients. Likewise, when you leave a company, sensitive inside information should not be shared. The world of design is small and if you get a reputation for a lack of integrity, it will be hard to find future work.

Similarly, taking care of details is an important skill to develop and become known for. To produce successful work, every area of detail needs to be examined as any flaws are likely to mean that the studio manager and/or client will reject the work. One of the characteristics of good design is that it is invisible: people notice bad design; people notice mistakes. This extends beyond the design project itself. When writing an email to a colleague or a client, check your spelling and reread it to make sure you are communicating what you intended. Sloppy emails will create the impression that you are sloppy at your work, which neither your boss nor your client will want to see.

Attention to detail

Attention to detail and the ability to communicate well are not developed in the same way as pure design skills. Communication and organization are very personal things, so find the methods best suited to your way of working, and the expectation of your clients and employers, and make a conscious decision to follow them.

For many people, simply taking a few minutes out to double check detail is enough, but if you know that spelling or proofreading is difficult for you, then ask colleagues to help. If your organizational skills are weak, there are a number of tools that can keep track of things for you and training courses to help you become better organized.

Photography

An understanding and appreciation of photography is a useful addition to your skill set because there will be a time when you cannot use stock photography and will have to commission and art direct photography. Most designers use a camera to shoot portfolio pictures, record research and inspiration, take preparatory images and much more. Whilst you don't need to be an expert to use an automatic digital camera, learning more about how a camera works and its capabilities will help inform your future photography decisions.

When working on a photo shoot, you may not be the one taking the pictures, but it is usual for a graphic designer to art direct it. As a designer, you should already have a keen eye for framing and composition and these skills will be used as you will have to ensure that the images taken serve the purpose for which they have been commissioned, because it is likely that you will have generated the design concept in which they will be used.

Post–production will also be the task of the graphic designer to perform color balance, cropping and retouching, and any other adjustments that are necessary to obtain the desired result.

MALMÖ FESTIVALEN FIRAR 30 ÅR! 15-22 augusti Gratis FÖR ALLA PUSS & KRAM

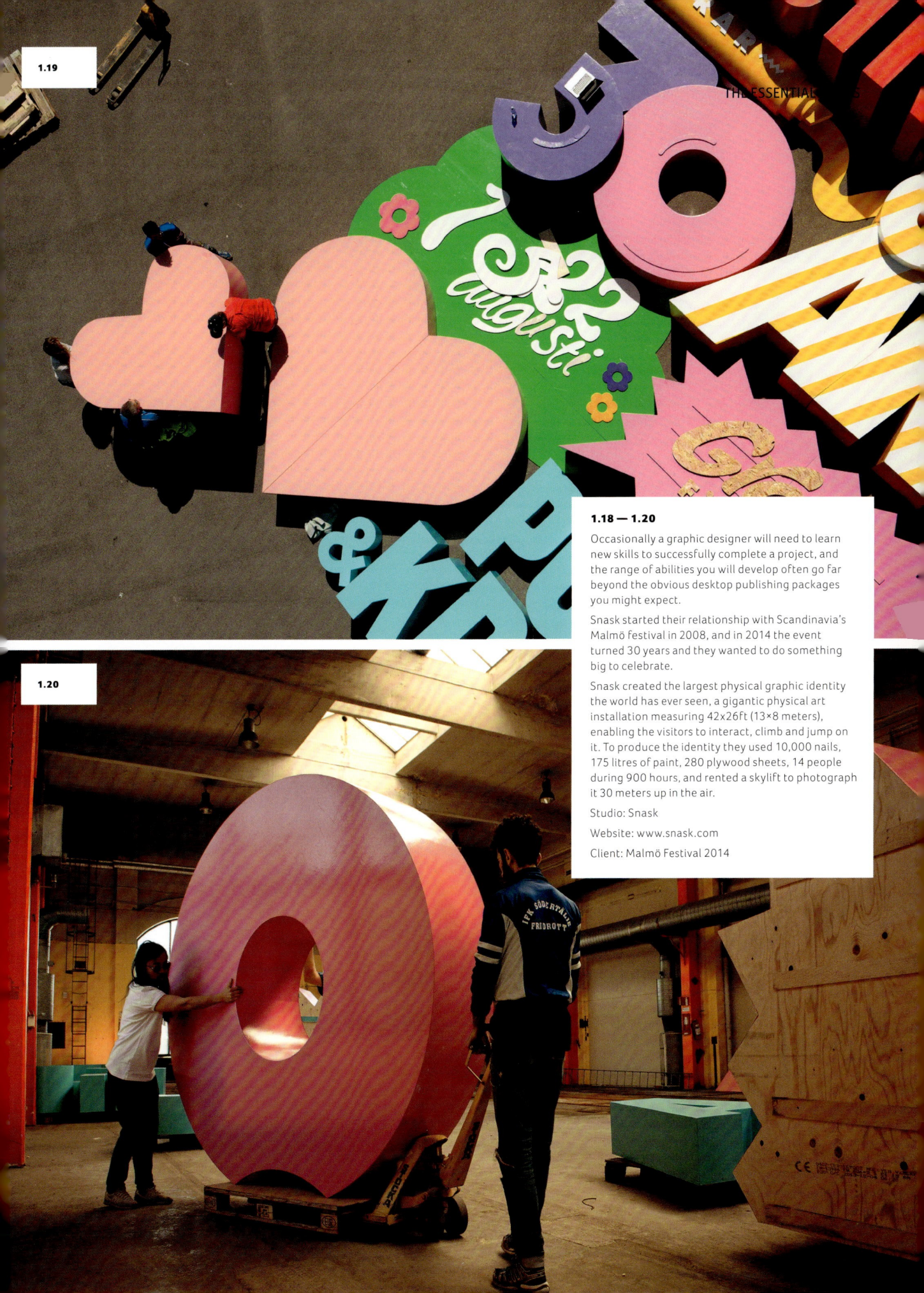

1.20

1.18 — 1.20

Occasionally a graphic designer will need to learn new skills to successfully complete a project, and the range of abilities you will develop often go far beyond the obvious desktop publishing packages you might expect.

Snask started their relationship with Scandinavia's Malmö festival in 2008, and in 2014 the event turned 30 years and they wanted to do something big to celebrate.

Snask created the largest physical graphic identity the world has ever seen, a gigantic physical art installation measuring 42x26ft (13×8 meters), enabling the visitors to interact, climb and jump on it. To produce the identity they used 10,000 nails, 175 litres of paint, 280 plywood sheets, 14 people during 900 hours, and rented a skylift to photograph it 30 meters up in the air.

Studio: Snask

Website: www.snask.com

Client: Malmö Festival 2014

Attitude

There are some fundamental expectations which are implicit, if not stated, about your role. Firstly, that you understand the briefing process and are able to deliver the services which you advertised, according to the client's needs. Secondly, that you will take responsibility in the creation of the work that is commissioned, and communicate with the client as required with the appropriate level of formality and respect. You will need to feel confident in the business and administrative processes that accompany a design project in order to work efficiently, effectively, and consistently as a designer. How you operate as a designer demands a particular attitude and approach that is pivotal to professionalism.

Professionalism

Professionalism can be thought of as a combination of general attributes that people expect you to have when doing business, such as reliability and good communication, being able to understand a brief and not deviate from it, being honest with the timing, keeping to deadlines and giving notice as early as possible of any issues.

Although design can sometimes seem like a solitary activity, particularly if you work freelance, you are actually working in an extended team that includes your client, their colleagues, their organizational client, professionals in other disciplines including photographers, illustrators, printers and so on, so you should aim to cultivate a broad professional outlook and adopt an appropriate manner throughout the operation of your business. A network is established and your contribution has an impact on this bigger organism and your ability to complete your obligations or not will have an impact on the livelihoods of many other people. Weaving reliability into your profile is essential for building and maintaining professional relationships.

Each client will communicate with you in their own way. It's likely that the phone call or email offering you a commission may seem casual and informal and the

dialogue friendly. Your aim as a designer is to respond appropriately whatever the approach and to develop an ongoing professional rapport with each client. Good communication should be two way — whether informing existing or potential clients of recent work or keeping your client informed of the progress of ideas for a specific commission, recognizing when you need to make contact, and how to do so, is a prerequisite of the job.

Confidence is essential. You have to project that you do indeed know what you purport to know and have the skills and abilities that you say you do. Although in the early days of your career you may feel like a novice, it's worth remembering that through inviting you to undertake a commission for money, the client is automatically placing upon you a professional status: you have been selected, which in itself is an endorsement of your authority to undertake the job. Be confident because confidence instills confidence. This means taking responsibility for pursuing opportunities, negotiating contracts, pushing the best solution to a creative problem and being firm when appropriate. Remember, however, that there is a distinction between confidence and arrogance.

1.21 — 1.24

A fourteen-page specimen of the typeface Scene by Sebastian Lester. Student Yu Rong used a time comparison approach to tell the story of the process used to develop the typeface.

Designer: Yu Rong

Website: www.yurongdesign.com

Instructor: David Hake, Academy of Art University

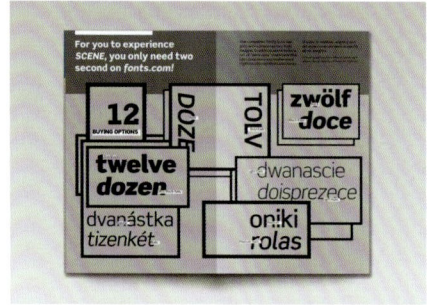

1.21

1.22

Pressing deadlines, the client constantly changing his or her mind after signing off the artwork and news that the printer cannot deliver on time are some of the sudden demands or unanticipated challenges that each commission brings. Remaining calm under pressure is a key success skill and one that will see you draw on your knowledge and professional experience to have the confidence that the job can be completed. To help manage and minimize sudden demands or unanticipated challenges, it is important that you establish the tone of your working relationships early on, so that people know that they cannot take advantage of your good nature, and so that you maintain your composure when resolving or overcoming problems. A client needs to feel confident that you are capable of achieving what is asked and any signs of anxiety or hysteria can cause the client and others that you have to work with to become stressed.

1.23

1.24

Developing your knowledge and staying ahead

Graphic design is not a static industry. Design theory continues to grow and tastes and preferences constantly ebb and flow — technology change is a constant. If you rely on the skills you learned five years ago, then you will be out of date, which means that you will have to continually invest time, effort, and sometimes money to develop and expand your knowledge. As a practicing graphic designer you will quickly realize that you need to develop a lifelong habit of learning, and this doesn't end when you graduate. If a day goes by when you haven't learned a single new thing, consider whether you are advancing your career.

Using the right tools for the job is essential and this means you need to constantly update your skills and learn new ones. For example, in a very short space of time, the culture of web design changed dramatically due to the increased use of mobile devices. New technologies, systems and working methods were introduced and several established processes became redundant overnight. A few years earlier, it would have been difficult to predict this sea change, so designers had to up–skill quickly or face losing clients. When the iPod and iPad were launched they were revolutionary. Now, in the age of smart phones that have large screens and large data storage capacities, they have become obsolete.

Taking time away from client work to generate your own projects is a good way to learn new skills and experiment with new ideas. Day–to–day work in a studio will help you develop and hone a certain set of skills, but if you want to change direction or learn something unrelated, this may not be the most conducive environment in which to do so, so taking time out or setting aside time at night or at weekends to develop new skills can help.

There are many ways to keep aware of developments and track new trends including blogs, magazines, conferences and networking. Invest both time and money to stay ahead. You'll need to make sure that you keep up to date with the latest equipment and software, but this is only part of the challenge. You should also be alert to new developments in technology. You can find tutorials online, attend courses, collaborate with others — get out, stay interested and curious.

1.25 — 1.27

The rebranding project for PIK NIK uses a combination of graphic icons, lines, bold and circles, to bring out random quirks in the food/drink menu. The result is a modern, fun identity, well suited to the client.

Studio: Oddds

Website: www.oddds.com

Clients: PIK NIK

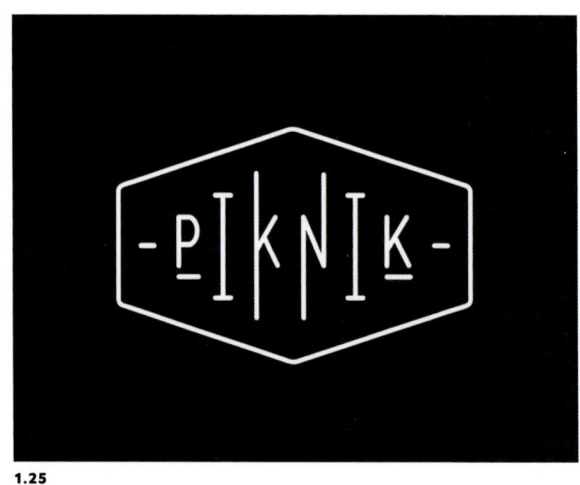

1.25

1.26

1.27

Magazines and blogs

There are a plethora of monthly, bimonthly and quarterly magazines available about design and the graphic arts and most design studios will maintain a library of magazines to help continue to educate and develop their designers, however, it is worthwhile taking one or two subscriptions to publications that address the particular field or discipline that you are interested in.

Blogs can also help the development of a designer. How–to blogs such as *Designmodo* teach you how to do specific things such as using different Photoshop or Illustrator techniques. Other blogs such as *Cool Hunting* or *Wallpaper** provide a forum for discussion and exchange of ideas — the blogger will usually be expressing their viewpoint or experience. And some blogs are simply a designer's or studio's electronic portfolio. Visual research blogs such as *Baubauhaus* provide research into a particular topic or theme, and blogs such as *You The Designer* provide a forum for new designers to showcase their talents. You are likely to find all types of blog useful to your work, and sometimes the sheer volume of information available can be overwhelming. You'll soon find out which blogs appeal most to you though, so sign up for updates and check–in regularly once you have your own shortlist.

Recommended design blogs:

www.friendsoftype.com
www.grafik.net
www.eyeondesign.aiga.org
www.itsnicethat.com
www.designspiration.net
www.aisleone.net
www.thefoxisblack.com
www.abduzeedo.com
www.thegreatdiscontent.com
www.formfiftyfive.com
www.css–tricks.com
www.thedieline.com
www.designsponge.com
www.thedsgnblog.com
www.smashingmagazine.com
www.designobserver.com
www.swiss–miss.com
www.typeforyou.org
www.notcot.org
www.design–milk.com
www.shillingtondesignblog.com
www.pjrvs.com/articles
www.creativeboom.com
www.typewolf.com
www.plentyofcolour.com

Recommended design magazines:

Creative Review
Desktop
I.D.
The Great Discontent
Wallpaper*
Web Designer
Adbusters
Bak
Media Graphics
Photoshop Creative
Communication Arts
Fuse
Print
Baseline
UPPERCASE
Desktop
Computer Arts
Computer Arts Projects
Creative Review
How
Layers Magazine
CMYK
Another Escape
Protein
Wrap

1.28 + 1.29

Revealing Craft, a photo book funded through a successful Kickstarter campaign, created in collaboration with photographer India Hobson & the online craft marketplace, Folksy.

Studio: du.st

Website: www. du.st

Client: Folksy

1.28

1.29

Design studio websites

Viewing the websites of leading design studios and graphic artists is a must for seeing how leading practitioners continue to push the boundaries of graphic design. Design studio websites also provide an excellent way of seeing what is happening in graphic design in different countries. There are far too many to list here but a good place to start are the following:

www.3deep.com.au
www.db–studio.co.uk
www.kellianderson.com
www.edfella.com
www.bantjes.com
www.katemoross.com
www.laverina.com
www.mousegraphics.gr
www.ogilvy.com
www.r–design.co.uk
www.manss.com
www.gavinambrose.com
www.ben–wout.nl
www.nbstudio.co.uk
www.researchstudios.com
www.seadesign.co.uk
www.thirteen.co.uk

www.thedivision.se
www.studiomyerscough.com
www.sagmesiterwalsh.com
www.muirmcneil.com
www.bobgilletc.com
www.alanfletcherarchive.com
www.chipkidd.com
www.jessicahische.is
www.pocopeople.com.au
www.socketstudios.com
www.kitchensinkstudios.com
www.lamoulade.com
www.yourlocalstudio.dk
www.madebyfieldwork.com
www.teacakedesign.com
www.stevenbonner.com
www.studiocontents.com

Conferences

Attending conferences can be stimulating and can expose you to new ideas and practices, as well as offering the opportunity of mixing with other dedicated people from your own and similar industries. There are many design events but some key ones include:

OFFSET
www.iloveoffset.com: A three–day creative conference with speakers from the worlds of graphic design, animation, illustration, advertising, film, fashion and beyond.

Generate
www.generateconf.com: Net magazine and Creative Bloq's conference for web designers and developers.

F5
www.f5fest.com: Brings together the thinkers and doers that are breaking ground and shaping new standards in media and design.

99U Conference
www.conference.99u.com: Focuses on shifting from idea generation to idea execution with action–oriented talks by leading creatives from numerous disciplines.

TYPO
www.typotalks.com: Design, culture, society — with a little bit of kerning

London Design Festival
www.londondesignfestival.com: An annual event that celebrates and promotes design in London.

AIGA
www.aiga.org/events: A range of events and lectures, hosted across the US.

D&AD
www.dandad.org: Student and industry awards, plus lectures and exhibitions.

What Design Can Do
www.whatdesigncando.com: An internationally focused event investigating the power of design as an agent for social renewal.

How Design Live
www.howdesignlive.com: Everything you need to know about pursuing a career in design.

Smashing Conference
www.smashingconf.com: New ideas and essential knowledge for designers.

1.30

Courses and online tutorials

As a graphic designer, you need to stay abreast of the latest developments in industry in terms of ideas and skills, but beyond this you absolutely need to keep an eye on wider cultural and political developments as these can have a meteoric effect on the way you work (a recession for example). Whether you use Twitter as a tracking tool, relevant periodicals, or RSS feeds, you should aim to learn something new every day and maintain a general overview as to what's going on.

Lynda
www.lynda.com: Great for step–by–step tutorials for anything from software to book keeping.

Skillshare
www.skillshare.com: A wonderful resource that allows you to learn direct from some of the graphic design greats.

YouTube
www.youtube.com: YouTube has everything. While there is little quality control, you'll find someone that's made a video talking your through your design problems.

Instagram
www.instagram.com: Though the videos are brief, there are tons of graphic designers using Instragram to show off their particular set of skills.

Teaching

Teaching can be a means of testing your current skills and sharing them with others, as well as developing your communication skills. While you may not want to become a full–time educator as soon as you graduate, you might consider guest lecture spots, part–time teaching, or running workshops for students. In addition to improving your presentation skills, you will also expand your design knowledge because students will push and challenge you in a very different way to clients. Students want to push the boundaries of the discipline as far as they can and are generally less concerned with limits imposed by the commercial world and peers.

1.30 + 1.31

Silicon Beach is an annual conference that takes place in Bournemouth on the United Kingdom's south coast. The event attracts leading strategic thinkers and digital innovators, from a wide variety of disciplines, all sharing their individual expertise and essential knowledge.

Website: www.siliconbeach.eu

1.31

Drawing and sketchbooks

No matter what part of the industry you work in, drawing will always be an essential tool. A sketch is still the quickest and most effective way to get an idea down or demonstrate it. If an idea is strong you should be able to sketch it out for the client; if it needs more explanation, then you have to reconsider it. By sketching out an idea, you can work through the concepts and consider things like proportion and scale before you reach for the computer. If you are roughing out a website design and want to be more precise, there are sketchbooks available with grids for browsers, and specific ratios for desktops, tablets and mobile devices.

Creating storyboards for film and animation sequences can be another great use of the sketchbook, letting you quickly judge things like flow and duration of scenes from a few simple marks drawn across a few frames. Storyboarding need not be limited to film and animation, the technique can be used for creating a plan for a project or mapping out the user journey of a website.

Sketchbooks and ideas books are also great places for experimentation and just recording stuff around you that you think is interesting. Keeping up a sketchbook or ideas book shouldn't be a chore, but rather an extension of your thinking. Your ideas can be recorded in note form, sketches of mind maps, drawings, and more. Carrying a sketchbook with you everywhere can be a good idea as you will never know when inspiration might strike and you want to be able to record these moments. When you are on the move it's a quick and easy way to record your ideas, plus it has the advantage of never running out of power and not requiring Wi–Fi.

Plotting and planning, sketching and collecting observations can sit comfortably alongside the odd doodle. Even if drawing isn't your thing, a sketchbook serves as your personal thinking space. Your marks probably won't be displayed in a gallery, and you don't even need to show these embryonic designs to your team, but this can be the best place to collect your ideas regardless of competency and drawing skill. Looking back through the sketch books you filled years ago will continue to inspire you and show you how your critical creative thinking has developed.

If sketchbooks really aren't your thing, there are some really good drawing programs for tablets, but the device will cost a bit more than a pen and pad…

1.32
Images of Clearleft's idea process and studio space.
Studio: Clearleft Ltd
Website: www.clearleft.com

1.33 + 1.34
Storyboards and sketches generated dung the UX London Workshop.
Studio: Clearleft Ltd
Website: www.clearleft.com

"Always carry a pen and pad. It's one of my best design tools, make notes and sketch initial ideas to make the design process easier."

Ricky Gane, freelance graphic designer, rickygane.eu

1.32

1.33

1.34

SPOTLIGHT ON... LISA HASSELL, INKYGOODNESS & WE ARE GOODNESS

Tell us a bit about yourself.

Currently I split my time between running our art and culture platform Inkygoodness and our newly formed creative agency WE ARE GOODNESS, representing illustrators and designers worldwide for commercial projects. I'm also a visiting lecturer and published writer, contributing articles to *Creative Review* and *Digital Arts* amongst others, and organize regular creative industry event Glug Birmingham.

You've done a lot of work to celebrate emerging talent and have provided many with a great platform to showcase their work. What inspired this career route, and how did you identify this need?

We had no grand plans when we started out. Inkygoodness was just a name we gave to an exhibition we curated, and then more artists wanted to get involved so we had a bigger one. We started to get some press interest and we were excited that people liked what we were doing. It felt like we were building a community, and the illustrators involved in the shows were super supportive, contributing towards the cost to make the shows happen. Our debut London exhibition in 2010 was a massive turning point. We had over 30 artists involved (McBess, Good Wives & Warriors and ColourBox to name a few). The gallery was packed out and the night ended with a cider–fuelled Space Hopper race down Brick Lane. It was a proud moment. We've since exhibited in Antwerp and Berlin (at Pictoplasma in 2012) but nothing matches the exhilaration of London.

In recent years we've focused our attention online, investing time in growing our online platform and connecting with international illustrators and artists.

How can emerging designers best make sure they stand out from the crowd?

Care, attention to detail, eye–catching design and a personal touch are qualities we value most. We get a tonne of submissions and the majority go straight in the trash, and not necessarily because the work is bad! I find it quite troubling that so many graduates still don't do their research before contacting companies. Addressing an email with "Dear Sir or Madam" or "Hello team" when the name of the director is clearly on the website is a sure fire way to get someone's back up. Basic manners also go a long way. If you don't hear back from a prospective client or magazine, a follow up email a week or so later is good. Calling the director's personal mobile three days in a row and leaving voice mail borders on stalking (yes this really happened).

How important is networking for designers, and do you have any tips?

For emerging designers still finding their way I always recommend getting a job in a café or bar. It might sound counter–productive but actually people–skills are half the battle when it comes to networking, and the more comfortable you are talking to strangers in any situation, the more confident you'll be to put these skills to the test when it counts. Attending creative events like Glug is also brilliant for young designers, as they're geared towards meeting new people. The atmosphere is friendly, relaxed and fun without being intimidating.

I think for any event it's important to have a goal in mind before you go — whether its striking up a conversation with a stranger, or handing out your business card to at least three potential clients. Social media continues to be an essential marketing tool for creatives too. Pinterest and Instagram are very popular tools for sourcing talent.

Freelancing is a subject you've covered often; there is always a debate as to whether students should get to know the industry before working for themselves, or jump right in. What are your thoughts?

There's no right or wrong way, and there are obvious pros and cons to both. Finding a permanent role is increasingly competitive, and I still feel there is a massive disparity between the level of skill students are equipped with upon graduating and the skills they need to secure a job in the creative industry. Internships can successfully bridge this gap, and I honestly believe that every design degree should make it a mandatory module. Until then the onus is on students to take full advantage of their term breaks to go out and get work experience wherever and however they can — even if it means staying on a friend's sofa for a month!

A number of designers you work with sell their own work direct to clients (posters, prints, etc.) as well as taking on commissions. Do you find this entrepreneurial behavior leads to more client work, or do you think for many emerging designers selling work of this type is a goal in itself?

Certainly for some individuals I'm sure that happens, but in the main I'd say it's probably not that common to land a commission as a result of having an online store. I think it's more to do with self–promotion and how the act of making and selling work can complement your freelance creative practice: free reign to test ideas and explore more experimental work without the constraints imposed by a client brief. Staying motivated can be tough for freelancers, so side projects like this can be a great way to burn off steam and keep creativity and ideas flowing.

1.35
In–store hand painted signage for Urban Outfitters, Leicester.
Designer: Alex Fowkes
Website: www.wearegoodness.com
Client: Urban Outfitters

1.35

SALT&WOOD

if

WE B

THE MERE TH

IN A WORD ITSELF, THAT HOLDS MORE VALUE T

"If" stems and orig
of huge massive
The ing
whether – the
In th

"If" becomes the
pure choic
undiscovered real

2.1 + 2.2

Salt & Wood is an experimental zine that collects manifestos and perspectives on topics of discussion.

Printed on uncoated paper, each issue is filled with a subject topic, photography, graphics and typography.

Studio: Oddds The New Anthropology

Website: www.oddds.com

Client: Self–initiated

UTTER BRILLIANCE

CHAPTER 2
THE PROFESSIONAL WORLD OF GRAPHIC DESIGN

In the final year of a graphic design course, a student is faced with a number of decisions to make about their future. A good graphic design course should have equipped you with the skills to enter the workplace in various different design roles, but there are also options open to you that aren't immediately obvious. In order to make the right choice about the career path you want to follow, it is a good idea to think about what you enjoyed most on the course in addition to what you were best at, as a career is a long time to do something that you may be proficient at but don't enjoy.

For example, if it is the practice of graphic design that you enjoy and the pressure of working to deadlines, then going into the industry is the right choice, although this decision will also have multiple outcomes and ways of entering the industry. For those who enjoyed the theoretical, academic and educational aspects, they can be explored further through undertaking a Masters degree program or even a PhD. Perhaps you might even choose to work in education as a lecturer, or as support staff in an educational environment.

2.2

In this chapter we will:

- *Talk about the differences between education and work.*
- *Identify who you might be designing for and how you might handle that relationship.*
- *Re–visit the design process and examine your role as graphic designer at each stage.*
- *Suggest ways in which you might like to try out different career options.*

The transition from education to work

Assuming that you want to enter the industry and practice as a graphic designer, there are two paths that people tend to follow: working for a design studio (or within a design department in a larger company), and working freelance. Often times they will change between these two modes throughout their careers for a variety of different reasons. Each mode has its advantages and its challenges and which mode is best for you will depend upon your aspirations and the kind of person you are as much as your design abilities. We examine these options in much greater detail in Chapters 5 and 6.

Whether working for a design studio or for yourself, the stakes are far higher in industry with commercial clients and there is a monetary cost associated with everything you do. Even the desk space given to you will cost the agency money and they will expect a return on the investment they are putting into paying for software, time spent mentoring you and just covering the expense of the recruitment process. Likewise, as a freelance, you will soon realize the effort it takes to earn the money to pay for the equipment you need and to keep the lights on in your house or apartment.

In college, a good project would result in a good grade; now good work may result in returning business and a growing client base and, through this, the money you earn. A mistake can mean that your company loses money, a commission and possibly even a client, or that you never hear from a client again and your reputation is sullied, making it even more difficult to obtain new business. Attention to detail and professionalism are therefore a must and are always your responsibility.

Similarly, whichever route you decide to take, the number of hours you have to work might be a shock to the system! Very few studios have a strict 9–5 schedule and you will be expected to put extra effort in to meet tight deadlines. As a new employee you need to ensure that you are not taken advantage of and you shouldn't feel that you need to be last to leave. One of the disadvantages of being a freelance working from home is that you have no work hours and this will often mean any time you are at home you are working, including weekends and holidays, because there is always work to do. Knowing when to take a break is essential to performing effectively.

The educational environment will typically give you assignments that allow you to explore your creativity. Commercial practice, however, often involves producing relatively routine pieces in a short space of time with little scope or budget for a dramatic creative solution. Forget the elaborate print finishing techniques and very cool visual effects on a website. Commercial clients frequently require simple things done well and cheaply.

2.4

2.3

2.3 — 2.6

"I didn't know my name until my mum wrote it on a banana" is a self–promotional set of screen–printed items including a jiffy bag, tote bag, double–sided print/résumé, note books, business cards and badges. The concept was to create a 'goodie bag' full of self–promotional screen–printed pieces.

Designer: Lilly Marfy

Website: www.cargocollective.com/lillymarfy

2.5

2.6

Your clients/commissioners

Clients and those who commission design work have specific requirements that they expect the designers they hire to meet, in large part because they have commitments to those that pay them or hire them. The basic requirements are for a job to be completed on time, on budget and to meet the brief given. Failure on any of these points is likely to result in an unhappy client and one that may not be disposed to send more work your way. Meeting these requirements, on the contrary, is likely to instill the feeling that the client can count on you, that you are dependable, and will likely lead to more work in the future.

Clients or commissioners have a specific message to communicate, which is why they have called on you, someone they think is expert enough to generate a solution for them. Sometimes a client will be knowledgeable about design and have a very clear idea of what they want, but frequently this is not the case. Most clients expect to be able to give a designer a brief, which could be vague or extremely detailed, receive some ideas after an allotted time and then the final result after another allotted time. They may not understand the mechanics of the design process or the difference between two different reds or two different fonts (although they might if it is important), but you should be prepared to explain and defend any design choice that you make. It is fair to say that clients expect excellence and zero mistakes, even if the budget is meager.

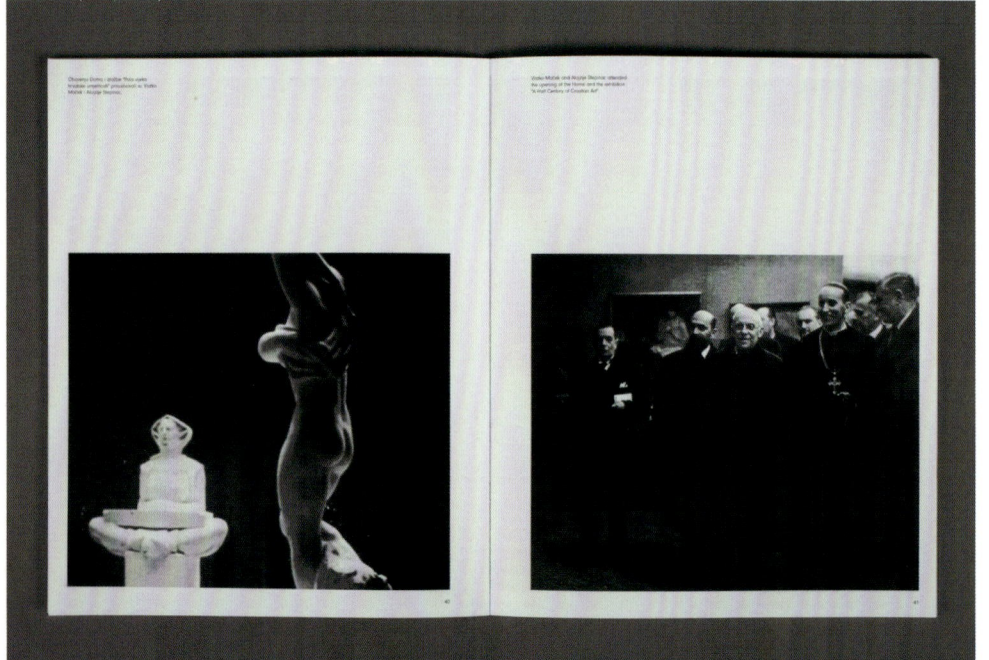

2.7

2.7 — 2.9

This publication explains a brief history of Croatian Society of Artists together with a photographic journey of a monumental pavilion designed by pre–eminent Croatian sculptor Ivan Meštrović in 1938. In World War II the building was converted into a mosque and in 1993 restored back to its original purpose. The pavilion is now used as an exhibition space for all forms of visual arts. The brochure created by Bunch consists of four covers showing different stages of the pavilion's history. Each cover is presented through die–cut circle reminiscent of the pavilion's form.

Studio: Bunch Design

Website: www.bunchdesign.com

Client: HDLU

Working with clients

Working with a client can be a smooth process, or a minefield — and the difference will depend largely on your approach and management of the client. There will be wonderful clients and terrible clients, but you need to give equal effort to each and every one of them. Sometimes the worst client will push you to create the best work. Clients expect clear communication, deadlines to be hit and good work to be delivered. Account managers handle most client contact, but as and when you have a direct relationship with them, you need to establish a way of communicating that works well for both of you, whether it is via periodic meetings, emails or phone calls. If you are going to take a client website offline to make changes, then tell them first so that they are not caught by surprise! Clients aren't designers and they do not need to know what a hexadecimal color is. Leave aside industry jargon and find a way to explain concepts that they will readily understand.

A client that emails constantly often indicates a lack of trust or understanding and a need to micromanage the process. You need to stress the importance of having the time to develop your ideas otherwise you will end up simply artworking their ideas. If a person is overly vague in their requirements it can be a sign that they do not know what they are looking for or they could be fishing for ideas. Over–communication can be as difficult to manage as under–communication, so set boundaries and contact times from the outset. If a client isn't willing to work with you on this, they may turn out to be a problem client. Disorganization is also a red flag. If they are continually late for meetings and don't provide necessary materials or information in a timely fashion, you can be certain they won't be paying your invoices on time.

Working with difficult and overly demanding clients can be extremely time consuming and can interfere with other work. The ideal client should have some experience of the design process, understand their own requirements, have an opinion and be open to suggestions. You can normally tell from your first meeting whether or not a client meets these requirements. A client who knows what they want will usually look for a designer who reflects their approach, so hopefully they will have approached you because of your specialism. Also, remember that working with clients and briefs that go beyond what you know will help you develop your abilities.

2.8

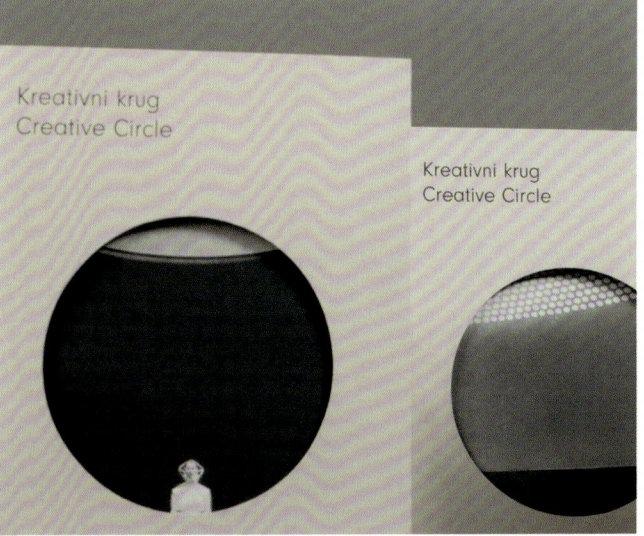

2.9

Holding the client's hand

Designers can see customer care as something that takes them away from productive creative time in the studio, but it is a skill to learn and develop. Your clients are your customers and they will want to feel engaged, appreciated and have some part in the design process. You also have to remember that clients look to you as the expert and may be hesitant when making decisions as the design process may be quite alien to them. Without hand holding, some clients will never make a decision, and if they do it will be a knee–jerk reaction in a bid to get something done quickly.

Imagine you are an estate agent trying to sell a house that has a terrible decor and no furniture, or you're trying to sell one that isn't even built yet. You would need to walk the potential buyer around, room by room (figuratively or literally depending on the scenario) and help them to picture how wonderful their life could be in the place. You will need to talk them through the details, the ways in which the space can be used, the modifications that could be made. This is how every design relationship with a client begins. You need to walk them through possible scenarios and look at how different options will play out over the long

term, what outcomes will appeal to which demographics and help them understand that informed change isn't a bad thing.

Whether it's their own money or the company's, a client will worry about costs and will need to know that results will follow. Reassuring them about your past successes or discussing well–known designs that have proven successful can instill confidence. Anything you (or the account manager) can do to assure them that they have made the right choice in asking you to take on the project will make the design process a smoother one.

> *"Be prepared to educate people about what you do, what skills a designer offers and what is better left to other professionals, why you can't use that copyrighted 72 dpi photo, and why adding animated characters to their website will make them look unprofessional."*
>
> **Monet Fort, Senior Graphic Designer, Professional Education at Georgia Institute of Technology**

WE DON'T HAVE MUCH BUDGET. BUT THERE WILL BE PLENTY OF WORK COMING YOUR WAY.

2.10

I AM JUST CALLING TO TELL YOU I AM ABOUT TO SEND YOU AN EMAIL.

2.11

2.10 — 2.13

The client is always right! is a self–initiated project created by STUDIOJQ. It may make you chuckle, it may make you scream, however this can be the reality of the design world. STUDIOJQ would like to stress not all of their clients are like this, just a small handful...

Studio: STUDIOJQ

Website: www.studiojq.co

The design process

The design process is a series of steps that designers take to successfully complete a design project. The process starts with the definition of the problem to be solved and the design brief. The design process aims to provide direction and control to a creative activity, and to steer the design team and client towards an appropriate solution to the design problem. Each project will be a different experience due to the nature of the material it concerns and the different people you will work with. You will find that while you take the lead on some projects, for others you will take more of a back seat, contributing to a specific area rather than the whole project. Hopefully you will have several projects on the go at once and so on any given day, you might find yourself working across multiple projects, at different stages with several different people. You'll be kept on your toes, but these experiences will help you to become a better designer and to grow as a professional.

For new designers, starting a project is an exhilarating prospect — you'll be applying the skills you have learnt, learning new skills, developing new concepts and sharing new ideas. But knowing where to begin, how to talk to the client, what to present at the pitch, and when to invoice for your services, can be daunting to start with. This knowledge will of course come with experience, but you can help yourself in the early days of your career by devising an approach to the design process that will suit you and your situation. This chapter looks at some of the ways to help you do this.

2.14 — 2.18

MTV needed a refresh of their corporate stationery kit, so they approached Motherbird with an open brief. The successful concept presented to MTV was the idea of photocopying each staff member doing something unique to them. A set of words were then produced, giving it that ultimate MTV cheeky feel. Each MTV staff member had two different photocopies and two words each, resulting in a rather big and bespoke print run that included four spot fluorescent inks.

Studio: Motherbird

Website: www.motherbird.com.au/

Client: MTV

2.14

2.15

2.16

2.17

2.18

Brief

Develop ideas & concepts

Present ideas & concepts to the client

Work with feedback

Present updated work to the client

Sign off ideas

Artworking

Present artwork to the client

Present updated work to the client

Sign off artwork

This diagram represents an ideal project workflow: the brief comes in, you work on a number of ideas and the client approves one. The winning idea is then artworked, presented to the client, refined, and then the project is marked as "complete".

This cycle may take place over a single day, or it may be several months depending on the type of job. However, you can guarantee that most jobs will not go this smoothly: clients will demand work is done "tomorrow" and some will lose confidence at the last minute and demand large concept changes, but that's the life of a graphic designer!

Client feedback

As often as a designer receives praise for their work they will also receive negative feedback. This can be due to many factors, and often it's not because they have supplied bad work, but more because the client does not have the terminology to pinpoint the areas of the project where they are not pleased. Working on a clear, concrete and descriptive set of terms with the client for discussing the work can really help the design process go more smoothly. As you are a creative, the client may try to use arty terminology to relate to you, but it is your job to steer them back to specifics. If they talk about 'feel', question them so you can understand exactly what they mean. 'Feel' is not a concrete term and can mean very different things to different people.

As the designer presenting the work it is your job to walk the client through the process, the thinking and the outcomes. You should explain to the client the reasoning behind your decisions and refer to solid research to support your decisions, using simple, clear terms. When discussing each point, ask the client for feedback and invite them to be part of the journey. The more engaged they are, the more constructive their feedback will be.

Feedback like 'I hate it' may be offered simply because they don't like a font or color choice, but can't separate this from the design as a whole. By discussing each part of the design, piece by piece, you invite the client to see each element as a contributing aspect. While you may have

firm reasons for your design choices, you will have to react to any client feedback, even if it is to prove that you are right. If you produce a blue logo and the client requests pink, do both designs and put them side by side. A client can often better understand your reasoning when they can see it for themselves. If you completely ignore their ideas and requests this will result in an antagonistic relationship and communication will become more difficult. Remember that you are providing a service and your client wants to feel that they are being listened to.

2.19

A page from the recently redeveloped Qatar Museums website. A collaboration between Qatar Museums, Wolff Olins and Cogapp, the site aims to encourage participation, nurture creativity, and showcase Qatar Museums' diverse projects.

Studio: Eleanor Rudge/Cogapp

Website: www.cogapp.com

Clients: Qatar Museums

"Listen to people. We all know design is about communication. In order to make sure my work is communicating the right message, I always make sure I listen to what everybody has to say. Understand the problem as best you can, ask questions, and listen."

Eleanor Rudge, www.flickr.com/photos/eleanorrudge

Top tips: Working to get positive feedback

It is fair to ask for feedback, and routinely you should do this. There may be simple points that you can address and these may help you win future work, but you will need to work with the client to ensure they can offer you the most useful insights.

- Research the client and get to know their business, then tailor your presentation to this.

- Prepare and practice, present to colleagues before the actual meeting.

- Make notes, but don't read from a script, as this will look unnatural.

- Make the presentation visual and exciting — if they are looking at the presentation, they won't be staring at you.

- Use research and demonstrate concrete metrics, a client will want to know exactly what effect your work will have on their business.

- Speak in a language the client understands and responds to.

- Don't be over-confident, and don't be too humble, as this will put people off.

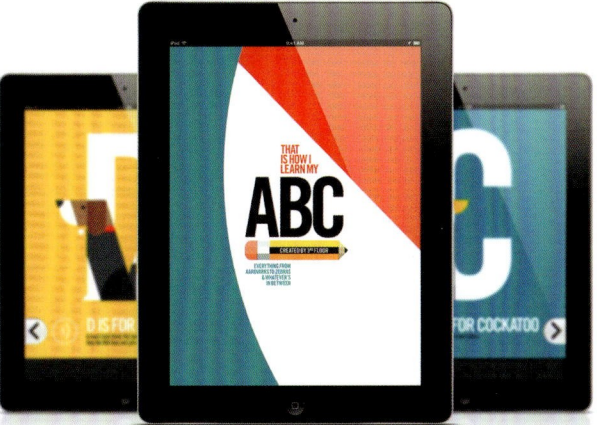

2.20 — 2.21

Self-initiated projects are a good way to demonstrate to a client that you can get it right, and that you know their audience. The ABC Project is an educational iPad application that features two games designed to help children to learn the different letters of the alphabet in a playful environment.

Studio: 3rd Floor

Website: www.3rd-floor.org

2.20   2.21

The brief

The brief is where the work starts. Many clients will come to you with a request and an idea of what they hope might be an outcome, but few will arrive with a fully formed brief. When a client asks for work to be undertaken, it is your first job to understand why they are asking for it and what the ultimate goal is. Asking critical questions will help you understand the client's requirements, and will enable you to develop a robust brief together. For example, a client may ask you to produce a brochure because "they need a brochure to increase sales", but critical questioning may reveal what they really need is a website with e–commerce capability. Design work often requires educating clients as to what they really need to achieve their objectives. Working with the client to structure the brief can be beneficial as you can bring your experience and knowledge to the situation — as an outsider you will devise an informed and structured response that gets to the heart of what the client really needs. Once you and the client have a clear understanding about the brief, you'll have a good idea of whether you can achieve the desired outcome working together.

A good brief will provide an overview of the context, the desired outcomes, budget and timescales. In addition to this, the client may offer examples of work that are similar to their desired outcomes (websites, logos, etc.), or if you are there to solve a problem, some insight into why their current approach isn't working and the issues their business is facing. You should always discuss areas of the brief where you need more information or have questions so that you fully understand what the client is looking for, and be sure to have the extent and scope of the brief confirmed in writing before you start work to avoid problems later on.

The best clients will allow you time to research their company and seek out the right actions and solutions, but often they will assess the problem internally and come to you with a set of proposed actions. This is why it is always useful to question their expectations and consider whether your work will meet these. If you believe the work you are asked to do will not offer a satisfactory outcome, it is best to say so up-front in a positive way and by offering suggestions that will help the client achieve their desired results.

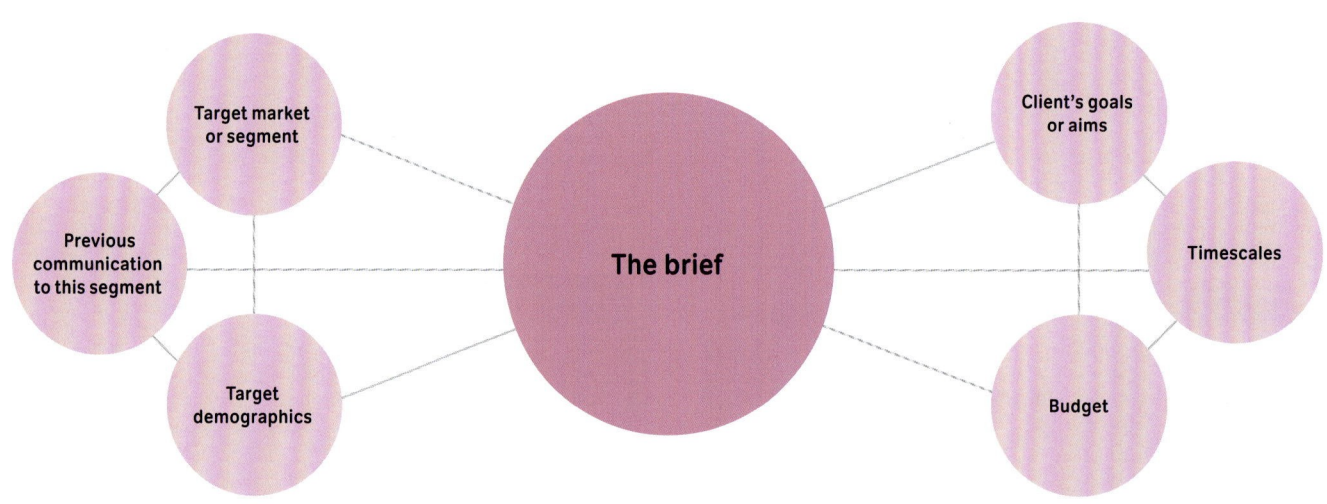

Previous communication to this segment · Target market or segment · Target demographics · **The brief** · Client's goals or aims · Timescales · Budget

Your creativity (or that of your employers) is the reason a brief has come your way, but ideas are only one factor when it comes to creating a successful outcome. It is vital that you are aware of anything that may impact your ideas or else they may be unachievable.

Your ideas may win the pitch, but are they achievable within the client's budget? Will the audience respond in a favorable way? Do you have the time to do the work? You should have some thoughts about these factors before you set pen to notebook.

Research

In education, design research is largely concerned with developing skills and an understanding of critical and contextual issues. This can be very inward looking and focused on the abilities of the designer. When a graduate enters industry they will quickly learn that research needs to be focused on others: the client, the context in which their business exists, the preferences of the decision makers and the target market.

Understanding the client, its business and their requirements is important for a successful outcome. This may involve looking into the history and origins of a business or company, to understand how it has developed and changed over the years, as well as how its branding has developed. For example, many companies now produce products and compete in sectors very different from when they were founded.

Beyond this you will need to get to grips with the larger context: which industry does your client work in, who are their competitors, who are their clients/customers and what are their expectations? A financial services company will have a very different view of the world to a technology company or a media company, for example.

Every project you take on will have a specific target audience. Regardless of what a client may tell you, an audience can never be "everyone". Such a statement shows that the client potentially lacks focus and may be a reason why they have a problem that needs fixing. If the brief relates to the launch of a new product or service, you may need to conduct some specific primary and secondary research to determine who the target audience is and what its attributes are.

It is likely that you can easily establish a clear primary audience, and you may also look to determine a secondary audience. The primary audience should be the major target, the group you need to appeal to most, however, it may not always be the person who controls buying behavior. For example, if you were advertising a new toy, the primary audience to appeal to would be children. But it is actually the parents (the secondary audience) who will make the purchase and so a design solution needs to appeal to them as well. You need to appeal to both parties and create solutions that say the right thing and don't exclude or alienate either group. Beyond the initial messaging to engage children, you may want to emphasize the safety aspects and any educational possibilities of the toy to get parents on side and comfortable with its purchase.

To help you set aside your own personal likes and dislikes from the design process and get inside the mind of the typical target customer, it can be useful to create a persona for your client's ideal customer, complete with demographic information. By giving this persona as much life as possible, you can reflect on what their needs, circumstances and lifestyle might be, thus providing possible insights into appropriate design solutions. For example, the typical purchaser of a sports drink might be a 23–year–old male, called Stephen, who has a job in the financial sector, lives in a rented flat, goes to the gym a lot, who likes rock music and is not interested in getting married yet.

Good research will help you achieve this and pencil in the attributes of the typical target customer, and in turn help you to more clearly explain your design decisions when presenting them to the client.

"How can you design something without a true understanding of who will be using it? Lets take a website for example, why would someone visit this website, what are they looking for, and what triggered their need? By understanding who those end users are, you can design something that answers their needs. Don't be afraid to challenge clients to adopt this user centred approach during your initial meetings — you'll end up with a thorough solution that you can be confident will please not only the client, but their customers too."

Jenny Coford, UX Researcher at Experience Solutions

This diagram details another way of looking at the brief–to–outcome process.

A designer will start a project by undertaking some research so that they understand the needs of the client and brief- before launching into idea generation.

Ideas developed at this stage are then considered in terms of viability and needs of the client. Those ideas that do not meet the requirements of the brief, client and audience are thrown out. The number of ideas decrease and eventually you are left with the right one: this is the process of synthesis.

Ideas are then realized as prototypes that are tested against criteria set in the brief (this may be anything from product durability to a particular audience responses).

These prototypes are refined, and from this the best possible outcome is developed.

Ideas

Research

Blue sky thinking

Ideation

Synthesis

Prototype

Test

Respond to feedback

Refinement

Outcome

Synthesis and development

You will probably start a project with an open design process in that you might choose to generate lots of ideas and potential solutions without worrying about specific details or constraints. This is commonly known as 'blue sky thinking'. Eventually, however, you will need to narrow down the possible solutions to ensure that you have one that is cost–effective and fit–for–purpose.

After the process of open idea generation has resulted in some realistic possibilities, these are then developed further. It is at this stage that you would normally start presenting roughly mocked–up ideas to the client to get feedback. In general, you might include some more inventive solutions along with some more mainstream and expected ones.

Once a design concept has been agreed with the client, you then have the task of refining it, offering color, layout, typographic and material options. Again, you will go through a process of considering various options, working towards an appropriate balance between the different design elements as you look to render your idea using the best possible graphic language. This involves using the material generated during the research stage and the target buyer persona to arrive at the precise color tone and typography that appeals to them and their lifestyle aspirations.

Delivering the brief

Once you have delivered your work and the client has judged it to have met their requirements and signed it off, for many people that marks the end point of a project. A successful outcome will be a design solution that meets the objectives of the initial brief and helps a client achieve their goals, although a design solution will often go beyond the original brief. The best designers are continual learners and for them the design process does not stop here. They will want to know how their design has performed and so will seek feedback from the client about how its sales have fared since the new design was used, and use this feedback as part of a review of the design process to see what worked and what didn't and try to answer why. Was there a design fault, an execution fault by the client, was the brief aiming at the wrong demographic, had something changed in the market?

Preparing for the world of work

As a new designer, it can be hugely helpful to "trial" various workplaces and set-ups. For many, work experience, internships, freelancing and mentoring schemes are the perfect opportunity to do just this — to find out more about their own strengths, weaknesses and career preferences. The availability of internships and work experience will depend on your geographical proximity to design firms, your contacts, skills, ambition and mostly, your confidence and effort in going out there and getting one. But if you can find one, chances are you'll find it hugely valuable.

2.22

2.23

2.24

2.22 — 2.24

Branding for London–based fashion, accessories, and art & design retailer, OTHER/shop.

Designer: Emily Hadden

Website: www.emilyhadden.com

Client: OTHER/shop

2.25

Emily Hadden's studio in Berlin.

Designer: Emily Hadden

Website: www.emilyhadden.com

Internships

Internships can be a great way to get into industry, especially if you are not sure which type of role might suit you best. The experience of an intern can vary widely from company to company, so choose your prospective employers wisely and ask questions of them. With so much reported through social media, it should be easy to find out about the experiences of previous interns. If this is not possible it may be worth seeking a few out and speaking to them. First, you'll want to find out whether you will be paid (at least expenses) and what you'll be expected to do. Ideally an intern will be placed into an environment where they can soak up the atmosphere, learn and build practical work experience on commercial projects. What does the employer get? They are a low–risk way for a potential employer to test your abilities and assess whether you fit into their company or not.

To obtain an internship with a design studio or in a design department may mean writing to them to see what intern opportunities exists and what the procedure for applying is or establishing a relationship with them in order to arrange work experience when you graduate. The use of creative self promotion items can pay dividends, as sending a standard résumé (see page 114 for more on structuring a résumé) won't get you noticed. However, a clever promotional piece might and could result in a phone call to come and see them.

The experience gained through an internship differs depending on the company and its requirements, ranging from hands–on project development work to performing menial or basic functions. Some internships are paid (this could be a full wage, token amount or travel expenses), while others are not. If you

are going to give your time as an intern (especially if you are not being paid) you need to carefully consider what you will get from doing so. If the experience is not likely to result in a job offer, then it might not be worth doing. However, internships provide the opportunity to gain experience working in a real work environment, to make contacts and get a feel for whether or not it is what you really want to do. An internship also provides the possibility of being in the right place at the right time should an opportunity arise, such as being able to fill in when another designer is sick or otherwise out of the office.

An intern shouldn't be expected to be productive in the same way an employee is and any employer should be aware that they are taking on interns to develop new talent, not just to get some cheap labor. There can be a fine line between being an

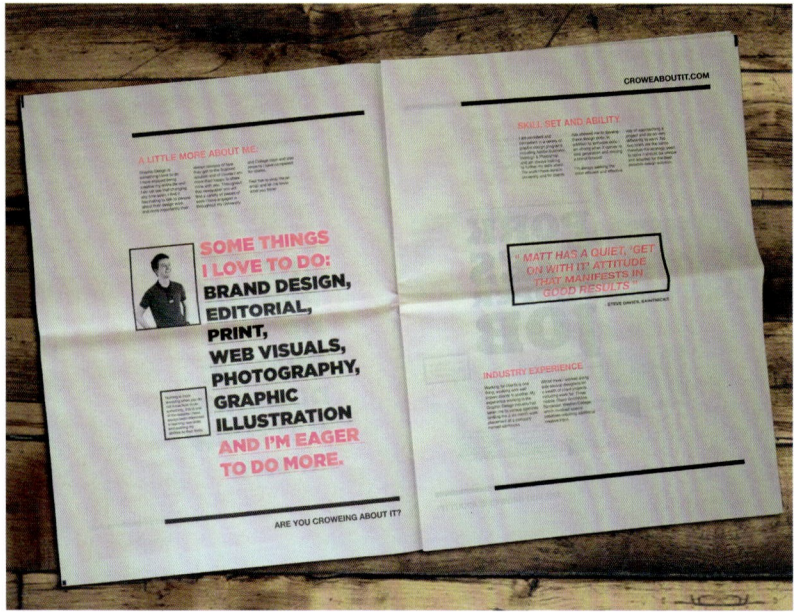

2.26

2.27

employee or an intern, and while it is good to be involved in a project (as you learn this way) an intern should never manage a project, work on a project unsupervised or be responsible for anything that is critical to the survival of the business (client or budget management for example). A company shouldn't expect an intern to be profitable as the idea of internship is giving someone the chance to prove themselves, and it is a time for the company to give something back and help an aspiring young designer.

An internship at a consumer magazine, for example, may involve participation in the editorial meetings to discuss the content and feel of the next issue, shadowing the art director to understand how photo shoots are directed and the visual aesthetic produced, being given a few pages of content to lay out and experimenting with

different layouts and configurations and discussing these with the head designer to learn what their strong and weak points are, and working with the production team to learn how the digital design files are transformed into the printing plates, and how the production run and finishing is handled.

When you are undertaking an internship, remember why you are there and what you need to get from the experience. Most people in a design agency understand the concept of internship and that you are there to get new experiences so don't be afraid to ask people for help or guidance, or to talk about their own career development, or tips for success. If you feel you need some guidance that you are not receiving, or you would like to know more about a particular area, then ask someone: a company should only take on an intern if they have capacity

for them, so you should never feel like a burden; just don't ask right on a project deadline! Perhaps keep a diary where you can note the projects you worked on, your contribution to them and the new skills you have learnt. Reviewing this at the end of your internship will allow you to see in which areas you have grown and strengthened and will certainly help you update you résumé.

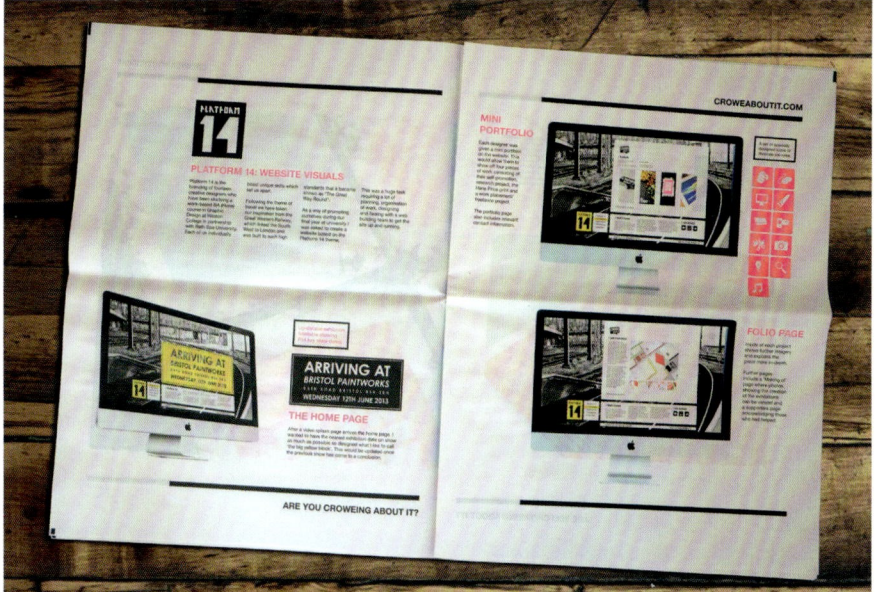

2.28

2.26 — 2.28

Self–promotion is crucial for a graphic designer, especially one starting out. To get noticed, Matt Crowe designed a portfolio which shows off his best work, but uses a non–traditional format — a newspaper. This tactic proved successful as Matt has now gained an internship and a number of freelance clients.

Designer: Matthew Crowe

Website: www.croweaboutit.com

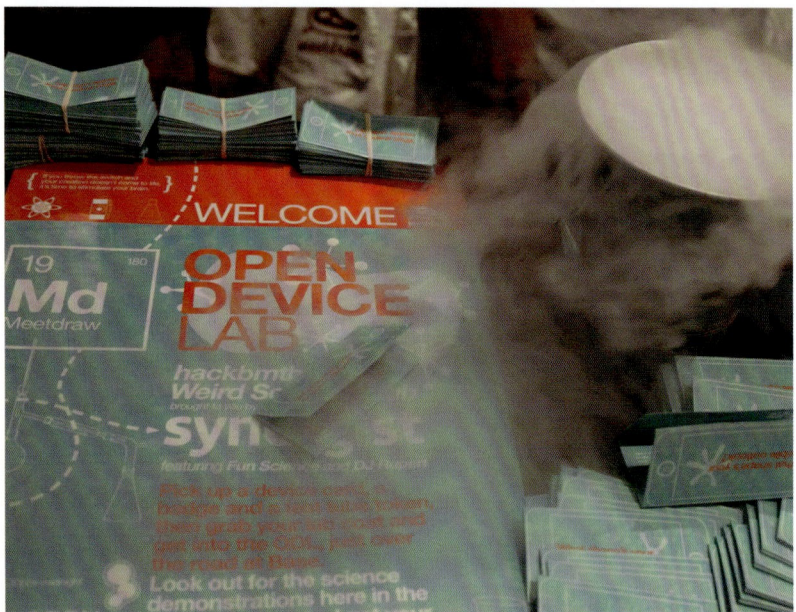

2.29

2.30

2.29 + 2.30

Meetdraw is a meeting of digital animals; together they talk about, and share collective passions, no matter what they do or what stage they are in their career.

Website: www.meetdraw.com

2.31

Design Buddy is a mentoring program that brings together industry experts and final year design students.

Across their last year of study, students are offered the opportunity to ask questions of someone working in the role they aspire to.

This innovative project created by Design South West, with the support of Universities South West and National Council for Graduate Entrepreneurship

Website: www.wedesignforum.co.uk/ projects/design–buddy/

Work experience

Work experience is similar to an internship in that it is usually unpaid or partially paid, and only for a defined period of time. It is also a very good opportunity to see if you like the company as well as for the company to decide if you are the right person for them. Work experience may be an option when you are in education or when there is a job opening and the employer wants to see how you will fare in a particular role. Work experience differs from an internship in that it is normally for a shorter period of time and it is

attached to one particular job role. While work experience is generally unpaid, it is likely that you will be expected to be as productive as other workers as it could ultimately lead to a paid job. As such, work experience can be viewed as a test in some ways.

There will always be lots of competition for internships and work experiences, as for many this is the best way to break into the industry and start a career in a nurturing environment while getting to work with big clients.

Mentoring schemes

Finding a mentor can really help. Learning the pitfalls from someone who knows the ropes can equip you with the skills you need to survive and prosper. While your mentor may not officially be named as such, it is good to have friends or contacts who know the industry, have experience and can guide you. Finding a mentor will often be an extension of networking and develop from a contact made at an event. This once again highlights the importance of cultivating relationships and presenting a good disposition.

Graduate freelancing

Many recent graduates will start their professional careers doing freelance work. This is great for those who are very motivated and just want to get out there and do it, and those that are good at self-promotion and networking. Many would prefer some experience prior to embarking on a freelance career, but if you feel that you have good business skills as well as design skills, this choice can offer you the freedom and variety of projects that an internship or work experience cannot. You can choose to work directly with your own clients, or in-house as a freelancer in a design firm. Chapter 6 discusses the life of a freelance in more detail.

2.31

SPOTLIGHT ON… BRUNO MAAG, DALTON MAAG

Dalton Maag has undergone a rapid growth (from seven to 55 staff) in quite a short period of time. How did this occur, and how did you cope?

In late 2009 we were approached by open source organization, Ubuntu, to design a font suite for their operating system. Working on an extensive project with an international technology company gave us a great platform to show our versatility, as it involved producing high–quality screen fonts in a variety of writing systems.

Not long after, Nokia came to us and asked us to look into creating a font to be part of their rebrand. It started off as a fairly big project, but limited to seven writing systems. When they saw how the font started developing and taking shape it was clear that what we had already done was just the beginning. Nokia began to realize the importance and impact that their font could have, and decided to expand it further and further. We were hiring up to three people a month to cope with the demand.

With type being such a specialized industry, it became a problem, to find the people. Many, though very talented, had neither had the experience nor were accustomed to working in the sort of environment that we had developed and to some extent we had to throw them in at the deep end, and at the same time provide ad hoc training.

From a legal and organizational point of view we needed structures. We needed to have to have HR, IT and other personnel who could support the designers to do their jobs efficiently. As your staff grows you have to adhere to legislation that would cripple a smaller company, so you have to bring in experts in fields other than design. Without this kind of support you simply don't have enough hours in the day to do what you are good at.

At Dalton Maag we are now 18 nationalities and speak 14 languages. This is very enriching and important. It broadens horizons and brings with it new challenges as well as opportunities.

For us, it was a really really fast growth and it was a hard time. It required us to reshape the entire outfit. There were many sleepless nights.

How do you recruit?

About half of our designers are from the Reading MA in Typeface Design course and there are a few people from the MA course in The Hague. Some of our people began as interns with the company, including our Creative Director, who joined us for three months initially. He was clearly very talented, so we offered him a job. He understood how the company worked, so developed his role quickly. He now leads our four creative teams made up of designers and technologists. Although our technologists are also type designers, they prefer the technical side to the drawing.

Now we train everyone to be multi–skilled; they may have a preference for either design or technology, but everyone should be able to work on all parts of a project.

Dalton Maag offers a training academy for new employees. Could you tell us more about the ethos and reasoning behind this?

The idea, and the absolute necessity for, an academy began to take shape because of what we had learned in our rapid growth period.

Every new recruit goes through the training academy, irrespective of where they come from. Depending on previous skills and experience, this can last from two to five months. This is for us to assess skills and identify where there is need for in–depth training. It also gives the trainee time to start thinking in the Dalton Maag way. We want to make sure everyone works in the same way and follows the same process so that at any point someone else can pick up any part of the project and understand what's been going on. The training allows us integration into the workflow, this is paying huge dividends and enables us to be more creative ultimately.

You have a great international reputation, how do you protect and develop this?

Check your work, and then check it again. It is all about quality and then maintaining that level of quality or even improving it. Working globally and with complex writing systems, we have to work with native speaking consultants that are from both design and linguistic backgrounds. We usually can get a complex font 95% right inhouse, and work with the consultants for the final 5%. Even when we are very familiar with the foreign writing system, we seek advice as part of our quality assurance procedures.

We try to keep up with local design trends in other parts of the world, as the visual expression of written language evolves at a rapid rate. We travel to conferences to directly get a flavor of developments and encourage our consultants to keep us informed also. Technology too plays a large part. In our part of the world we talk about the latest smartphones. The reality is, however, that in China and India smartphones are only just starting to become popular. The vast majority of people still use low–end devices, and Nokia is still strong in that market, selling easily 100 million units a year.

A font like the Nokia one you designed will be used by millions of people on a day–to–day basis, how does this feel?

It's really exciting to create type for cultures that don't have the typographic evolution that the Latin script has experienced. Gutenberg's innovations in the development of moveable type, which

was to industrialize and popularize information and knowledge, transformed European society completely. That simply didn't happen elsewhere. With industrialization you need rationalization, leading to simplification of character shapes. Many complex scripts never underwent this kind of simplification. In some parts of the world printing with moveable type wasn't introduced until the mid1800s and because of the complexity of some writing systems, type design and typography is not as diverse as we experience it to be. Today's computer systems are slowly changing this and cultures who use complex scripts are looking at simplification, too.

This is an important step, to realize that calligraphy and typography are two separate disciplines. They can live harmoniously side–by–side and inform each other.

You have a process of reflection after every brief for your designers. Why is this offered and how do you feel it affects your business?

Sometimes the complexity of a project demands that we immerse ourselves in research on particular aspects of that project, for example, the rendering technologies on specific devices before even a single character is drawn. The research is not a substitute, however, for reflection on the work done, which identifies potential skills and training needs. Reviewing the work with your peers is an essential part of personal and professional growth, as well as an opportunity to share experiences with the business as a whole and to learn from mistakes.

When projects are planned we aim to give our font developers variety in their work. Providing a break in a six–month project, by, for example, moving a designer onto a small logo refinement for a couple of days, helps the individual to refresh their eyes and their thinking about the project. It is also an opportunity to just step back and see if something could be done differently to affect the outcome more positively.

SPOTLIGHT ON… BRUNO MAAG, DALTON MAAG

What inspires you?

I am a trained typesetter. I did an apprenticeship in Switzerland for four years and from when I first walked into the print shop I knew it was what I was going to do. I love the atmosphere; being able to print something, seeing it there in front of you, and for it to be used the next day. Before that I had never had any exposure to typography because in my family no one is from a graphics background. My family were all mechanical engineers and I tried an apprenticeship in this to begin with. I didn't enjoy it and it was my mum that suggested I try something different, like the printing industry.

Later I went to Basel School of Design to immerse myself in designing with typography, as typesetting is more of a technical process. I wanted to learn design skills and be able to make design decisions. After the initial year of typography I continued with another three years of studying visual communications. This was a broader design course that included typography, semiotics and film studies, among other disciplines.

However, it was always the letterforms that fascinated me, and to this day my life is black and white, curves and straight lines.

At Dalton Maag you see your staff as craftspeople more than designers. Where do you see this distinction, and how does it affect your work?

Although I am a creative, a designer, I see type design as a craft discipline. Yes, I do create solutions to a problem, and answer a brief given to me, which is a design process. Even a library font design fulfills a specific purpose. It is the execution of the work, that every curve is right, that each kern pair is appropriate; that usability, accessibility and functionality have been carefully considered and catered for. That is craft.

When you are designing for a font library and there is not a client, how do you decide where to start?

We look at various things like the gaps in our font library, we talk to colleagues in the industry to find out what they require and respond to that. Sometimes you may doodle a few letters and then assess whether the development justifies the investment, not just in monetary terms but in publicity and contribution to the library. Our workflow demands that conceptual decisions, such as the size of a font family, are addressed. A serif may only need Regular, Bold and Italics whilst a sans must have more weights and styles.

Dalton Maag offers a wonderful internship program, and this seems to be key to what you offer as a company.

The one thing I believe in passionately is to invest in people who work with us by providing continuous training, and to provide opportunities to people who have an interest in type design. We continuously host interns. I believe that it is important to give someone a chance to broaden their skills and experience. But being an intern should be about learning and experiencing an industry, not being used as cheap labor. We support our interns with living costs where appropriate, and they work on their own projects. We do not expect interns to be part of our production process. They have access to all of our resources and should we access their skills we will then pay them normal wages as I don't believe anyone should work unpaid.

Internship needs to be a learning experience so that the young person can make an informed decision about what they would like to do with their lives. I was lucky when I was young to have been given opportunities to expand my professional horizon and to help me form my career. It's not getting easier for the younger generation to establish themselves in a fast changing world, and I see it as my civic duty to repay the kindness and guidance that I was given.

2.32

2.32

Dalton Maag's London studio.

Studio: Dalton Maag

Website: www.daltonmaag.com

SPOTLIGHT ON… JAMIE SERGEANT, CROWD

Tell us a bit about yourself.

Crowd is a creative communications agency with one simple mission: to build the crowd that's relevant to you with ideas born from intelligent insight, technical expertise and raw creative talent. We do this across all media platforms, all technologies, and all sectors, ensuring our clients get the right solution every single time.

How does Crowd work?

Crowd is a talent incubator. We offer paid internships and a chance to work with global brands and a highly experienced team in a safe environment. Students are mentored and work part–time alongside their studies. They will work on a range of projects, so we help them find their passion.

How have the students that you've worked with developed?

A sense of professionalism is instilled and developed quickly when students work with us. As they are working on live projects, there is a rapid growth and through this they will develop new skills, both professionally and technically. Most importantly, they will have an agency environment to add to their résumé and this experience can help a lot when they are applying for jobs.

You worked on a number of exciting projects with companies that are located across several countries. As you are a reasonably new and small team how have you managed to grow so quickly and how do you attract such a varied array of clients?

Networking is key to the growth of any agency and pro–actively developing a client base. Putting yourself in the right place and talking to the right people is the best way to bring in new and exciting project.

You can't rely on people finding you, but we do get a good number of enquiries through our website.

Winning awards helps get the name out there and spending any extra time working on projects to really showcase what we are capable of show the strengths of the agency.

The business model you've adopted allows you to be manoeuvrable and responsive to client needs (almost a "collective"), what inspired this approach?

Wanting to work with the very best talent and most passionate individuals within the industry inspired our business model. Having the resource to produce a message that works across all mediums is a very attractive proposition creatively. To achieve this, we work with many practitioners from many disciplines, including film, illustration, graphics and more. Mostly, we enjoy what we do and that's key to our success and continued growth.

What do you look for in a student or recent graduate?

Apart from a great portfolio we look for a strong web presence, as this is our business. Social media is a great way of showing off your work and reaching an audience.

We expect candidates to have researched our company (or any other they apply to). They should have an informed opinion and be able to talk about their favorite work by the agency. Above all else, they need to have a positive approach and be able to demonstrate a willingness to learn.

What are the main challenges design agencies (of all sizes) face?

Creating a company culture where staff are happy is key to success. Getting people in with the right skills is

2.33

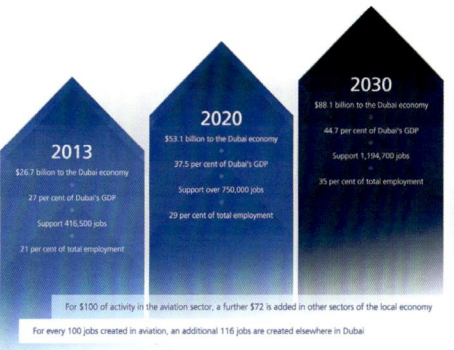

2.34

2.35

always a challenge and our model ensures we work with a wide range of talent. Managing the workflow can be a challenge and maintaining relationships with clients.

The range of projects needs to be a fine balance between those that are creatively rewarding and ones that ensure the wages can be paid.

How do you measure success?

You are only as good as your last project, so try and make it better than the last. Good work leads to more good work, and this leads to good money. In order to develop your business you need to concentrate on the growth of your network. As the business grows you will need new offices and equipment to cater for this, so from the outset you need to instill the right company culture and look out for opportunities, leads and industry awards.

2.33 + 2.34

Crowd devised a digital strategy to transform Dubai Airports' annual report into a digital only publication.

They utilized video and animation to highlight key facts and figures rather than relying on standard graphs and charts; by taking this innovative and unique approach they created an engaging and award winning experience.

Studio: Crowd

Website: www.thisiscrowd.com

Client: Dubai Airports

2.35

Crowd's Bournemouth office.

Studio: Crowd

Website: www.thisiscrowd.com

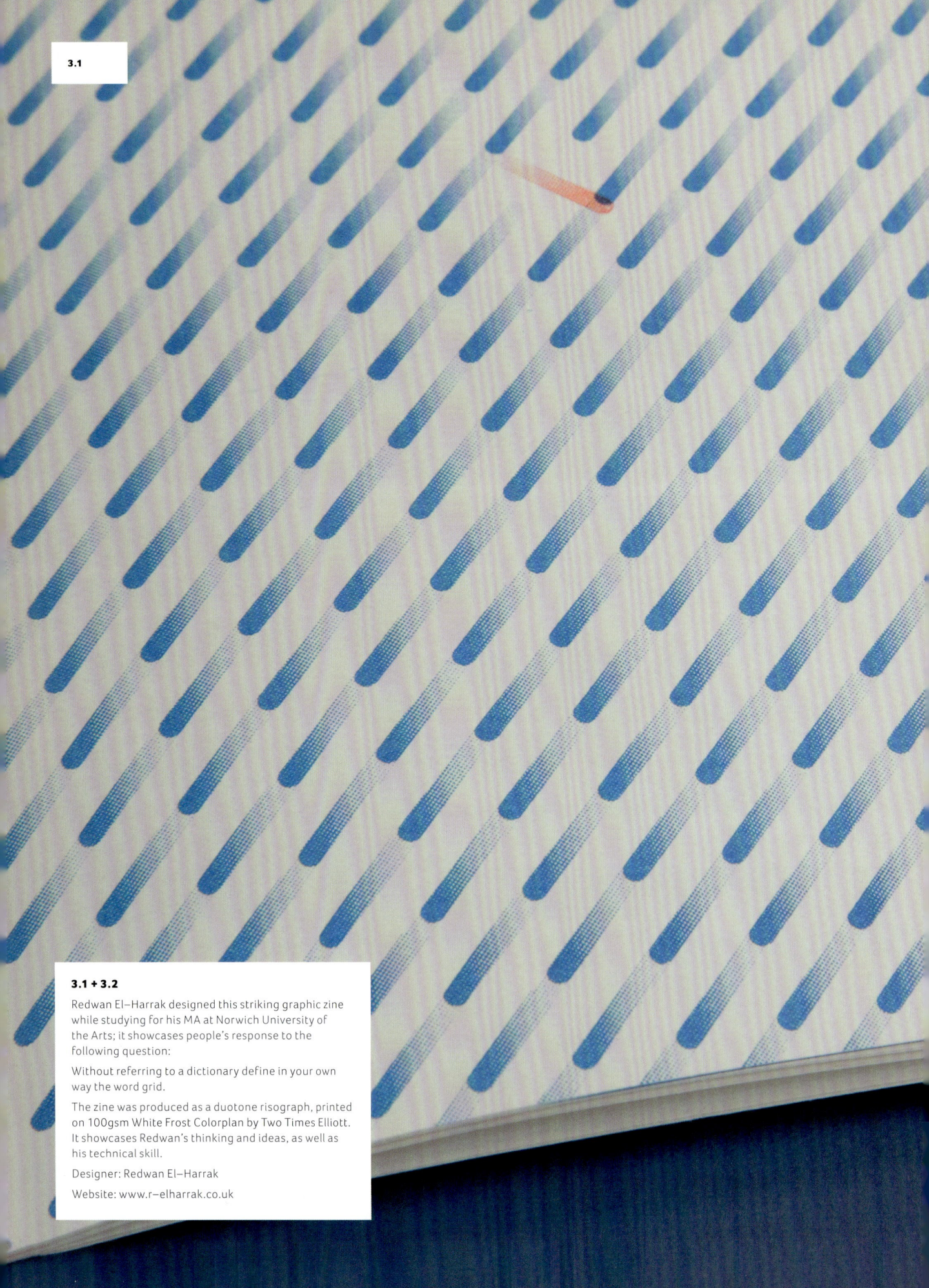

3.1 + 3.2

Redwan El—Harrak designed this striking graphic zine while studying for his MA at Norwich University of the Arts; it showcases people's response to the following question:

Without referring to a dictionary define in your own way the word grid.

The zine was produced as a duotone risograph, printed on 100gsm White Frost Colorplan by Two Times Elliott. It showcases Redwan's thinking and ideas, as well as his technical skill.

Designer: Redwan El—Harrak

Website: www.r—elharrak.co.uk

CHAPTER 3
GETTING OUT THERE, AND GETTING NOTICED

Getting noticed is all about getting ahead of the pack and showing off your skills and abilities. Business cards and other promotional materials are useful tools, but these are only a part of your campaign to get work. Marketing, promotion and networking are essential elements for making useful contacts, but be discriminating and targeted when making choices: research and find the right opportunities, and then focus your efforts there.

3.2

Columns and Rows

In this chapter we will:

* *Help you to establish who you are as a designer and what it is that you are selling.*

* *Suggest ways in which you can tell potential customers about yourself and what you do.*

* *Discuss how to compile and present your portfolio.*

Your personal brand

To develop your personal brand you really need to go through the same steps that you would to create a brand for a product or company. A well thought out brand will help you stand out from the crowd of other aspiring designers. This doesn't need to be overdone, but your promotional materials must look professional and should reflect your skills as a designer. The design principles you learned at design college or school apply equally to the materials you create to promote yourself and generate work, for example a consistent color palette and controlled usage of typeface styles will make your self–promotion look like more of a concerted and coherent effort.

Create a design brief for a marketing project for yourself and approach it in the same way that you would a commercial job. Define well what the purpose is. Are you trying to get a job or obtain work? Do some research about yourself and work out what your own unique selling point (USP) is, so that you have a realistic understanding of what you can offer to a potential employer or client. Is your strength and passion in magazine layouts or packaging design, websites or digital animation?

3.3 — 3.5

Jonathan Mont is a Mexican designer; he is a lover of branding, the creative process and the effect that it can cause. He uses ingenuity, function and intuition to create design that connects with people. His striking personal branding wholly embodies this ethos.

Designer: Jonathan Mont

Website: www.jonathanmont.com

3.3

3.4

3.5

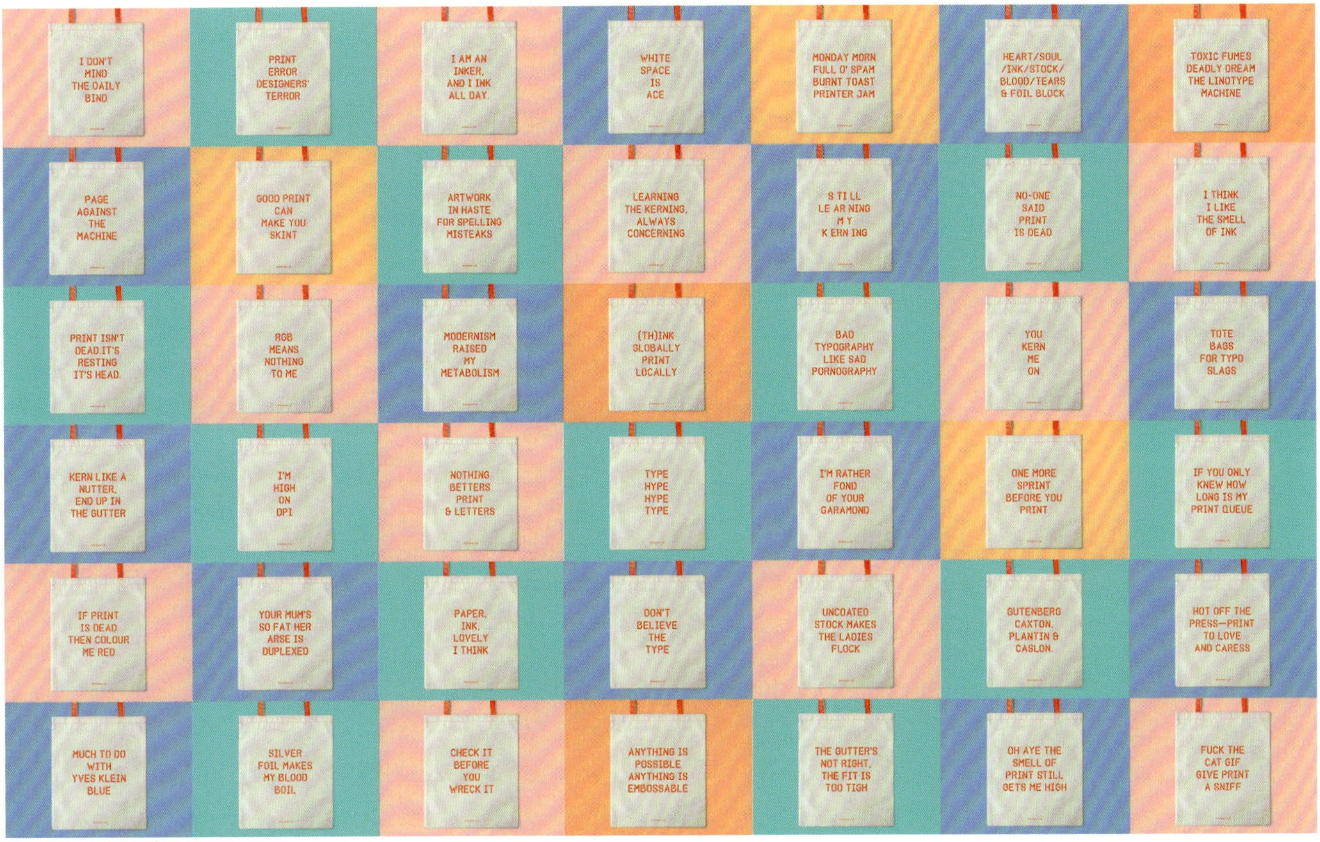

I DON'T MIND THE DAILY BIND	PRINT ERROR DESIGNERS' TERROR	I AM AN INKER, AND I INK ALL DAY.	WHITE SPACE IS ACE	MONDAY MORN FULL O' SPAM BURNT TOAST PRINTER JAM	HEART/SOUL /INK/STOCK/ BLOOD/TEARS & FOIL BLOCK	TOXIC FUMES DEADLY DREAM THE LINOTYPE MACHINE
PAGE AGAINST THE MACHINE	GOOD PRINT CAN MAKE YOU SKINT	ARTWORK IN HASTE FOR SPELLING MISTEAKS	LEARNING THE KERNING, ALWAYS CONCERNING	S TI LL LE AR NING M Y K ERN ING	NO-ONE SAID PRINT IS DEAD	I THINK I LIKE THE SMELL OF INK
PRINT ISN'T DEAD IT'S RESTING IT'S HEAD.	RGB MEANS NOTHING TO ME	MODERNISM RAISED MY METABOLISM	(TH)INK GLOBALLY PRINT LOCALLY	BAD TYPOGRAPHY LIKE SAD PORNOGRAPHY	YOU KERN ME ON	TOTE BAGS FOR TYPO SLAGS
KERN LIKE A NUTTER, END UP IN THE GUTTER	I'M HIGH ON DPI	NOTHING BETTERS PRINT & LETTERS	TYPE HYPE HYPE TYPE	I'M RATHER FOND OF YOUR GARAMOND	ONE MORE SPRINT BEFORE YOU PRINT	IF YOU ONLY KNEW HOW LONG IS MY PRINT QUEUE
IF PRINT IS DEAD THEN COLOUR ME RED	YOUR MUM'S SO FAT HER ARSE IS DUPLEXED	PAPER, INK, LOVELY I THINK	DON'T BELIEVE THE TYPE	UNCOATED STOCK MAKES THE LADIES FLOCK	GUTENBERG CAXTON, PLANTIN & CASLON.	HOT OFF THE PRESS—PRINT TO LOVE AND CARESS
MUCH TO DO WITH YVES KLEIN BLUE	SILVER FOIL MAKES MY BLOOD 'BOIL	CHECK IT BEFORE YOU WRECK IT	ANYTHING IS POSSIBLE ANYTHING IS EMBOSSABLE	THE GUTTER'S NOT RIGHT, THE FIT IS TOO TIGH	OH AYE THE SMELL OF PRINT STILL GETS ME HIGH	FUCK THE CAT GIF GIVE PRINT A SNIFF

3.6

3.7

3.8

Identifying your strengths and weaknesses

A simple business tool called SWOT analysis can help you determine what your strengths and weaknesses are. SWOT means Strengths, Weaknesses, Opportunities and Threats and is presented as a 2 x 2 grid. SWOT doesn't mean being the teacher's pet, but it does mean being honest with yourself. The first two boxes look at you: What are your strengths? What are your weaknesses? You may be a good illustrator or have a knack for using typography or white creatively. Conversely, you may not be adept at programming or creating animations. By determining whether specific design skills are strengths or weaknesses for you will help you to focus on the things that you are good at, and possibly seek to improve those that you are not so good at.

The opportunities and threats boxes look at the market environment and help you identify where are likely to be the strongest possibilities of obtaining work. A look at job advertisements and speaking to design studios will give you an idea of the skills that people are looking for. For example, digital design continues to evolve and grow whilst many traditional print–based forms of design are contracting. If your strength is working with letterpress, a technology that has largely been supplanted by digital printing and lithographic methods, it may be better to focus on improving some of your other skills where there are likely to be more work opportunities, unless you are confident that you can turn it into an opportunity, such as specialist printing for corporate invitations.

3.6 — 3.8

Print Poetry was launched in collaboration with Cerovski and Hyperactive. The project aims to get creative juices flowing by asking designers to enter print–related rhymes. The winning entries win tote bags with winning rhymes printed on them.

Entering competitions can be a great way of determining where your strengths and weaknesses lie.

Studio: Bunch Design

Website: www.bunchdesign.com

Client: Cerovski Print Boutique

Strengths

What are you really good at?

What skills do you have that will help you stand out from the crowd?

Weaknesses

Are there skills or attributes that you don't currently possess? For example, are job advertisements asking for skills you don't have?

Opportunities

Are there weaknesses that you can turn into opportunities by seeking training or advice? Alternatively, are there avenues you have not explored yet?

Threats

Are there external factors that may affect your chances of employment, or progression such as economic instability? You may not be able to fix these threats, but awareness will help you plan.

Creating an identity

Once you have a better idea of who you are and what your strengths are, and the skills that the market is looking for (the opportunities), then you can work on marketing yourself. Develop some messaging concepts about yourself, or what is known as an elevator pitch — a 30–second description of who you are, what your skills are and why you're the best person for the job. Practicing and refining your pitch will help you explain more clearly and effectively what you know and how you might be able to help the person you are speaking to. No one wants to hear "I do a bit of this, and sometimes a bit of that…" Be focused: being vague and general does not sound confident and lacks clarity. Concise communication about your abilities and experience will make you come across as a clear thinker and sound more professional, which is often what people are looking for.

There are various tools that you can use to show your abilities and your approach to work, such as business cards, letterhead,

a website and portfolio or showreel. Remember that whichever element you produce, you are creating branded communications about yourself and so the content, design and style of these tools must reflect your brand and be consistent across different items.

As you work in the field of graphics, a website, electronic portfolio, CD or showreel will probably be your most important promotional tool. In addition to carrying your brand, the content of such tools should reinforce the brand. Do not include everything you have ever done on your website or showreel. Pick a handful of the pieces of work that best show your technical and commercial abilities. Remember the Minimalist principle of "less is more". Be focused, direct and meaningful. If you cannot decide what to include and what to leave out, look at your SWOT analysis again and focus on work that reflects your strengths and the opportunities that you are seeking.

You will need to create a brand identity to use on your website and other materials that you produce such as business cards, letterhead and envelopes. A good, well–considered brand identity will be a natural conversation starter at networking events and interviews in addition to displaying your design skills to potential clients and employers. You may email people with a link to your website, or you may also choose to post a CD–ROM with a digital portfolio or showreel. This approach has the added benefit of placing a physical object in the hands of the recipient and provides an opportunity to catch their attention with the envelope design or packaging it is sent in. Get creative with your self–promotional items.

3.9 — 3.11

March is a collaboration of architects and creative marketing professionals. The core mission of March is to build brand value through architecture.

Following a renaming to March, a new brand and visual identity was developed to complement the strength of the name. Using basic elements, layouts, and grid, the goal was to create a structured, organized appearance that reminds of architectural aesthetics.

This idea of transparency was used in the stationery, as March practices and develops architectural solutions that prioritize client brand needs over architectural style.

Designer: Zivan Rosic

Website: www.zivanrosic.com

Client: March Studio

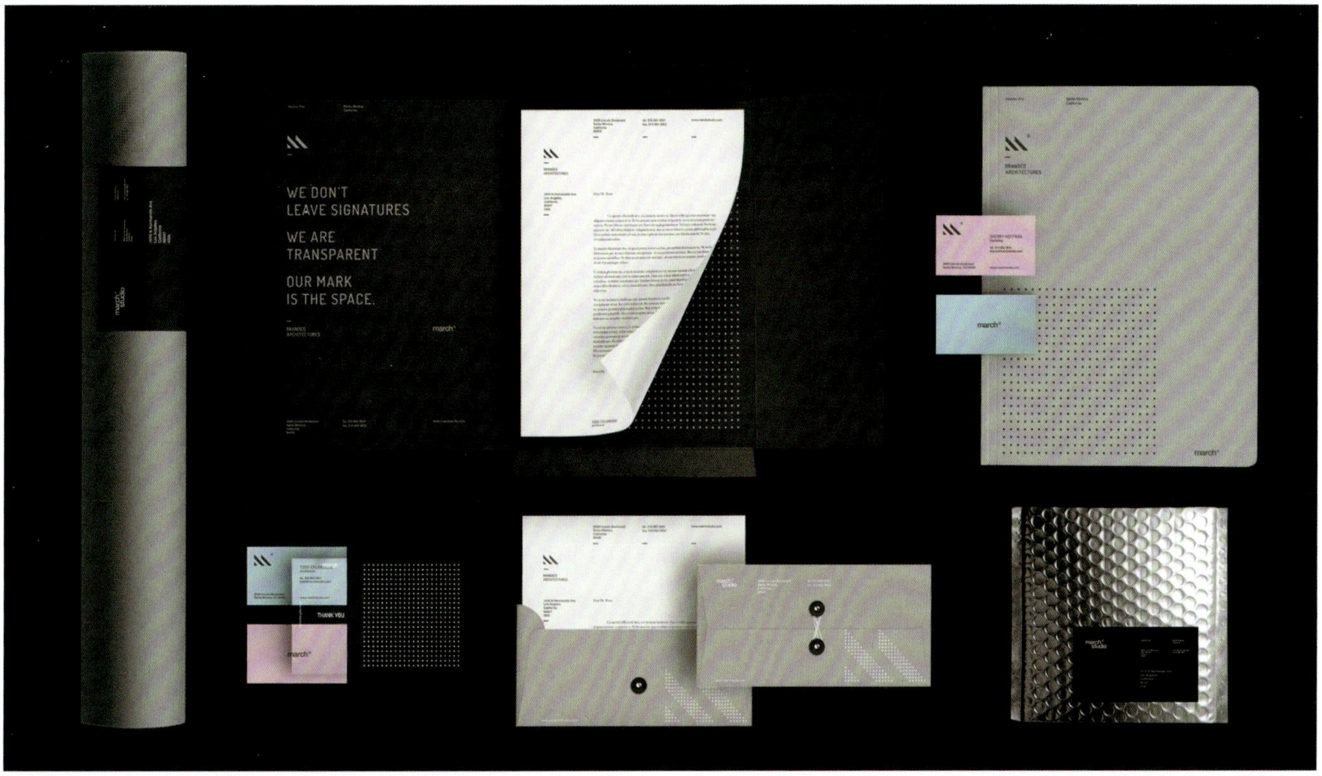

3.9

3.10

3.11

SPOTLIGHT ON… JESSICA WALSH, SAGMEISTER & WALSH

Tell us a bit about yourself.

Hello! Well, my name is Jessica, and I live in New York. I am a multidisciplinary designer interested in creating emotional and concept–driven work with beautiful form. I always try to approach the process in a playful way with a sense of humor. I want people who view my work to experience or feel something: whether it makes them think, brings them joy, or inspires. Our studio Sagmeister & Walsh works on a wide range of design from branding, commercials, advertising, book design, illustrations, products, packaging, to installations and exhibitions.

You've developed a number of self–initiated projects such as 40 Days of Dating and Quotes on Shit. Do you find these projects affect your client work, and do they help you in terms of promotion? Sagmeister & Walsh is a fairly small team, but you have some high–profile clients. Is this challenging, or does working with a small team allow you to take more risks?

I think personal projects are extremely important to me to balance with the client work, and I always have a few I am working on at any one time. It allows me time to play and experiment and take more risks. This is when I create my best new ideas and processes, and these discoveries often feed back into my client work. The personal projects also can help widen your audience, which in turn can lead to new client work.

You have a very entrepreneurial approach and have made the most of opportunities afforded to you (from an early age!). Others may struggle to take the same risks or see the opportunities a situation offers. Do you have any advice for them? Did you feel your education prepared you for your chosen career, or are there lessons you wish you'd learnt earlier?

One piece of advice I can give is to stay persistent. Getting to a good place in your chosen creative career takes insane amounts of hard work and passion and it is not an easy path. I personally hit many bumps along the way. I've seen people be successful from all types of backgrounds be successful at all kinds of creative work, both as specialists or more generalists, across all kinds of creative disciplines. From what I've seen it has much less to do with education, and much more to do with your persistence and attitude. There's also the component of risk taking, as you said, but that can be calculated. It just takes some common sense to be able to evaluate opportunities given your skill set and life situations and make the best moves to help you get to where you want to be.

You were an intern at Pentagram and Print magazine prior to your current position. Did this experience help you choose the right path and do you feel internships are the best way to break into the industry?

Yes, these experiences were crucial in helping me to determine what I wanted to do and the paths to take. I can't say that an internship is always the best way into the industry, it depends on your situation.

How did it feel to form the partnership Sagmeister & Walsh at 25?

I had been working with Stefan at his studio for two and a half years, and we worked together very well. In 2012, we started to have conversations about how we could continue to collaborate in a way that was mutually beneficial for the both of us. I was already in charge of most of the client work at the studio, and had been thinking of starting my own studio so that I could get recognition for the work I was doing. Stefan was interested in spending more time on the studio's self–initiated projects like "The Happy Film". We worked out a partnership which allows us to do both things, and help each other both out in the process.

Of all the lessons you've learned through your career, what advice would you offer to a student looking for their first job?

Early on, I suggest trying not to worry so much about making a huge paycheck right away, especially if you are right out of school and have a lot to learn. When you are young you should find studios or designers you really admire, and try to work and learn from them. Try to find your creative voice and show your personality in whatever kind of work you are doing. Work hard, do the type of work you love doing, and stay passionate and persistent. Lastly, use common sense to evaluate and know your worth, and speak up for what you feel you deserve.

3.12 — 3.14

Function Engineering specializes in mechanical design and engineering for product development within, but not limited to, consumer electronics, computing and networking, mobile, medical, robotics, entertainment, commercial and industrial equipment.

They approached Sagmeister & Walsh to create a new brand identity system. Narrowing in on Function's expertise in designing hinge & linkage mechanisms, they designed a typographic system based on a hinge/pivot system. They expanded on the system by creating a series of icons, illustrations, and patterns which can be used flexibly across various collateral in print and online.

Studio: Sagmeister & Walsh

Website: www.sagmeisterwalsh.com

Client: Function Engineering

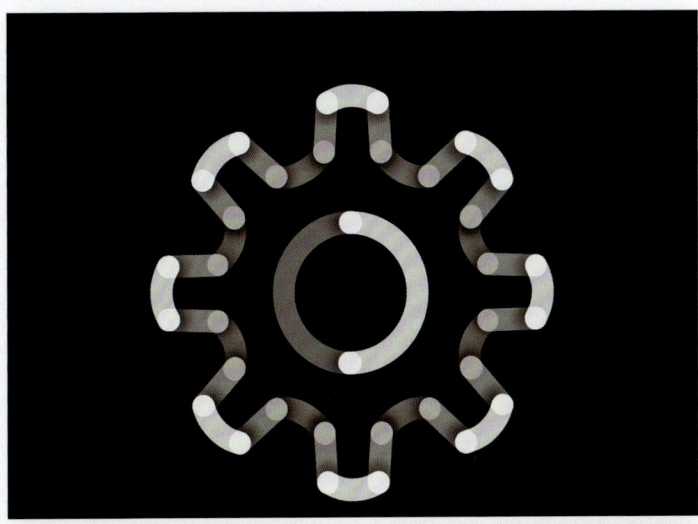

3.12

3.13

3.14

Promoting yourself

Creative self-promotion includes a wide range of activities, from those that are targeted to those that are almost frivolous. The important thing is for them to help build your brand by showing off your creative abilities. It goes without saying that in addition to promoting your work, self-promotion methods must provide your contact details so that interested people know how to get in touch with you.

Self-promotion is a constant activity for many designers, particularly those that work as freelancers due to the constant need to win new work. However, you don't have to wait until you graduate to begin promoting yourself. The best time to start self-promoting is while you are still in education. As well as providing the opportunity to start generating relationships with potential future employers and clients, education often also provides a greater opportunity to create pure design pieces, rather than the applied design work that dominates much of professional practice. People in industry are also much more willing to give students a helping hand, guidance or work experience, which can help when building contacts, a résumé and a portfolio.

Going beyond standard self-promotion takes more effort but the results can help you build a new audience for yourself and distinguish yourself from other designers.

Websites and blogs

Every creative person needs a web portfolio or blog to showcase their work and/or discuss their work approach. Some designers use a formal website while others use Tumblr, Wordpress or other web-hosted sharing software to host an electronic portfolio of commercial work. Needless to say, if the USP that you offer the market is web design, your website should be sleek, functional and should showcase some of the dynamic web tools that you are adept at using. Apply the same restraint as for your physical portfolio and show only good work and don't pad. An online portfolio will normally have more work than its print counterpart, so think of ways that projects can be divided into sections so that the user can navigate them easily. Need help? Look at the websites of design studios and see how they manage their online portfolios.

SEO (search engine optimization) is something you need to pay attention to if you wish to be found online as there are thousands of design graduates looking for work and if "graphic designer, graduate" are the only keywords you are concentrating on, then you will never be found amongst the competition. Fortunately, there are many strong keywords that you can utilize by simply putting together a thorough "about me" page. If you describe who you are, your geographic location, what you do and your skills, this information will naturally generate a number of good keywords. Each project in your portfolio should also be properly captioned with a brief description: project name, client, aims and objectives, key skills demonstrated and a link to the work in context where possible.

Social media and promotion

Social media is key to getting design work. Through the provision of platforms such as Tumblr, Dribble or Behance, you can show that you are active and provide an opportunity to display your work in progress. Posting designs in social media allows you to show more than you put in your portfolio but some judgment needs to be exercised as well. Doodles, works–in–progress and sketches of ideas can complement your finished pieces and show your thought processes and how you generate ideas, which others may find interesting (or not).

Actively participate in discussion groups or comment on blogs created by other people to let the world know that you exist, and to share your knowledge and expertise. By actively posting your opinions on hot topics and examples of your work, there is the possibility of it being reposted or linked to on other blogs, and you may also catch the interest of potential employers or clients. For this reason, you should keep your linked social media accounts reasonably professional.

Social media also provides an opportunity to find out more and relate to people in organizations who you would like to work for or with. Many positions are no longer advertised via traditional routes such as newspapers or magazines as this costs a lot of money, takes time and is not always the most direct route to the right person. Companies often ask for recommendations for new designers or freelancers from those they currently use, and you have to be part of this audience in order to be able to jump in and offer your services.

If you want to work for a company, follow them on any social media outlets they might have so that you can conduct research into them and keep up–to–date with their news, views and ideas. Companies often announce vacancies via their social media feeds, so following them means you will be one of the first to know about potential opportunities. Connecting with people who work in industry or specific companies via LinkedIn for example, and joining relevant discussion groups, also provides the opportunity to share your knowledge and ideas in a space that is likely to be seen by possible employers. And, if work should come up in the future, they may be able to recommend you, so it is useful to build bridges and talk to them about their projects, work in progress and the skills required.

Postcards, CDs and packaging

Traditional methods of self–promotion such as postcards, flyers, CDs and eye–catching packaging are still relevant self–promotion tools, particularly when used to promote an event or happening that you are taking part in. Although creation and distribution of these physical pieces has a cost, they all provide the opportunity of putting something memorable in the hands of someone you aspire to work with. Such giveaways need to present the essence of what you are about and what your USP is. If you create something that the recipient wants to keep on their desk or put on their notice board, you may well be the first person that they call when an opportunity opens up.

Pop-up galleries

You can curate your own show or pop-up gallery. Organizing such events can be remarkably easy, and normally the hardest thing is finding the right space. Renting a gallery can be expensive, so think about other places that people go such as cafes, bars and other public spaces where the managers may be inclined to offer space for short periods of time without the hassle of contracts (in return getting a few more people than usual through the door). Providing some free refreshment (purchased from the person offering the space) will help interest people in coming, and you can spread the word across industry using social media and email lists that you have built up from contacts you have made.

Like any event, it will need to be well branded and promoted effectively if you want people to hear about it and, more importantly, come. Don't rely solely on social media: send invites to the people that you want to come along as many potential attendees will not move in the same social media circles as you do. Write to local agencies and freelancers directly to invite them to your event, but when you do ensure you have a clear message and reason for them to attend. Are you going to market your event as a social occasion or as an opportunity for agencies to discover new talent or an opportunity to purchase original pieces?

Self-generated projects and competitions

Self-generated projects provide the opportunity for you to design the ideal project and showcase the extent of your talents. If you have a passion for typeface design, don't wait for a client to request one. Instead create the typeface that you want to make and post it or sell it online. Before long, you'll generate a reputation for being a typeface designer and that will start the flow of work to come your way.

Entering competitions can be a good way to gain exposure: even if you don't win, getting shortlisted will generate some publicity for you and the feedback from the judges, in addition to the competitive atmosphere in general, will help you hone and refine your skills. Winning prizes is great for promoting your work and worth listing on your website as it proves your expertise to potential clients and employers. Competitions you may wish to enter include:

D&AD:
www.dandad.org

International Society of Typographic Designers:
www.istd.org.uk

YCN:
www.ycn.org

Adobe Awards:
www.adobeawards.com

RSA Student Awards:
www.sda.thersa.org

Design Week Awards:
www.awards.designweek.co.uk

HOW Design Awards:
www.howdesign.com/design-competitions

3.15

Sumi is a self-generated student project while Sue studied at Plymouth College of Art; the work went on to win "Best in Show" at D&AD. The creative challenge was to launch a conceptual and predominately visual fashion brand from concept to completion. Sue combines the immediacy of the web with the tactile experience of print, aiming to stimulate new ways to engage across online and physical worlds. She generates ideas by blending techniques in moving image, photography, typography, printmaking, laser-cutting and digital design.

Designer: Sue Lewry

Website: www.suelewry.com

Your portfolio

A digital or physical portfolio is your main tool in obtaining work as it will showcase the best of your abilities in a concise and succinct way. A good portfolio will demonstrate real talent and personality, and it will help the viewer understand what they can expect if they hire you.

While you may have great creative ideas, potential clients and employers want to see examples of current commercial work so get them in as soon as you can as this transmits expertise and professionalism, and shows that you can work in the real world to real deadlines and budgets. Your prospective employer has limited time available and will not wade through page after page, so you'll need to self edit to focus on your strengths. A rule of thumb is to include only eight to fifteen projects.

This helps show that you are focused, a trait all employers want to see.

Of course, the type of designer you are (or want to be) will determine the type of portfolio you put together. As a print designer, for example, you will probably want to include work that demonstrates your knowledge of printing, production techniques and special printing effects. As a web or interactive designer, an electronic portfolio might be more suitable. Or as an advertising designer you might want to demonstrate their commercial potential while animators and illustrators might take a more artistic approach. Build the portfolio that feels right for you and what you want to do.

The work contained in your portfolio should be specific to the interview and the position you are applying for. However, as a guide you should look to demonstrate:

- Examples of creative thinking, research and idea generation

- An overview of your technical skills and ability

- Projects relevant to the position you are applying for

3.16 — 3.18

Doug Hindson's portfolio represents the culmination of three years studying illustration and animation at Kingston University. Doug wanted to make a portfolio that reflected his multidisciplinary approach and love for physical materials.

Designer: Doug Hindson

Website: www.doughindson.com

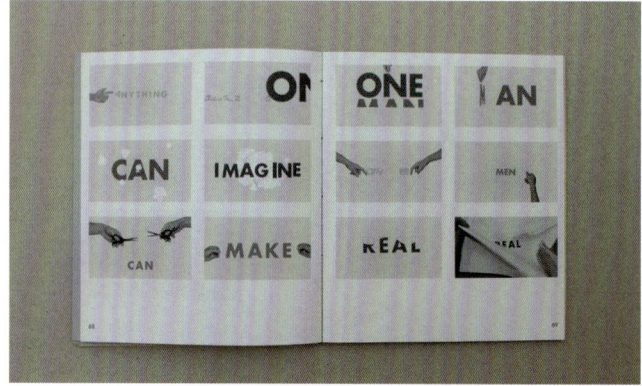

3.17

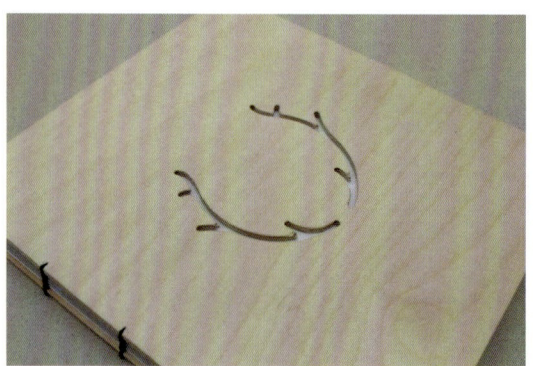

3.16

"Take the time to finish your online portfolio, it's better to have a few projects that you can reference than having to say you are just working on it. A portfolio will never be finished, but be passionate about the work you have done and clearly articulate why you think it's good. Show sketches and the thought process as well."

Jamie, This is Crowd

Your potential

Even if you have not undertaken a live brief with a client, work developed in education will showcase your potential. While it may be worth noting that it is student work, don't worry that it is not live as the employer can still determine potential from the way you have worked to a brief, developed concepts and executed the final piece. Beyond this you may look to include work answering completion briefs, self–generated projects, and anything else that shows you have the skill and ability to make creative graphic design work.

Commercial potential

When a studio hires you, it will cost them money. The employer will invest a great deal of money in your workspace, computer, software, mentoring and occasionally training. They need to know that they will get a return on their investment, and that you have the ability to hit the ground running. To prove this you should look to include examples of work that you have done for clients, projects undertaken while on work experience, and anything else that shows you can meet the requirements of a commercial project and deliver suitable work, to deadline, and within the budget.

Skills

The portfolio is your chance to show either a range of skills, or one particular thing you are excellent at (again this will depend largely on the position you are applying for). However, remember skills are not just technical processes, you need to showcase your ability to generate innovative concepts, communicate effectively with clients, and think creatively.

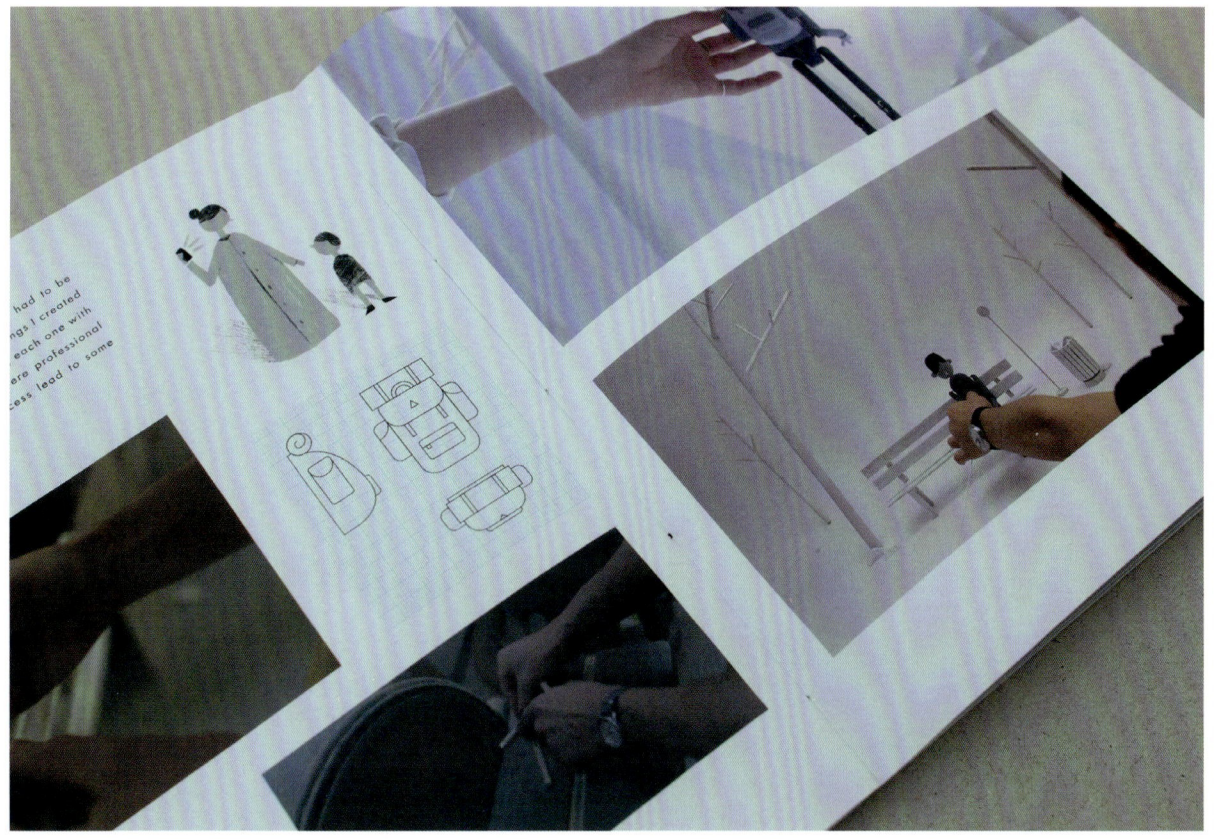

Demonstrating your process

Aside from final artwork, you may also want to include work that shows your process. Sketchbooks can be a really good way of doing this and you may include one in the back of your portfolio. To paint a fuller picture of you as a practitioner, you may also want to include links to a blog and/or social media if this demonstrates your ability to engage with current debates and cultural ideas. A visually rich blog and Pinterest account can show your influences and show the employer that you are looking at the right stuff.

What to leave out of your portfolio

Occasionally you will find yourself wanting to showcase a piece of work in your portfolio, but be unable to do so due to restrictions on copyright, or because you've signed an NDA (non–disclosure agreement).

When a job is won you should know from the outset which party will retain the copyright of the final artwork. If the copyright is to reside with the client, you will have to ask their permission before you show anyone else the work or include it in your portfolio.

Similarly, an NDA means that you are not able to show the work, but the restrictions are slightly different. Normally an NDA protects a concept before it is launched and restricts you from talking about the project with outside parties until it is out in the world. When the work is launched you should be able to detail your involvement, depending on copyright ownership.

How you've been hired to do the work will also affect the ability to show projects in your portfolio. If you've been subcontracted to do work it is better to keep this quiet, as it can look bad to employers if their clients think the work has been done in–house.

There are other considerations more to do with fairness; for example, if your current employer has trusted you with their best clients, is it okay to use this work to get a new job? Largely, most companies will understand that employees move on and will not restrict their ability to show off work they have been involved in, but they might not be too happy if you are using this to apply for work with a direct competitor, or if you are looking to take the client with you.

3.19 — 3.21

Graphic designer, Jen Devonshire's identity and portfolio website. A designers website says a lot about them and this example clearly reflects Jen's personality, ability, interests and diverse skill base.
Designer: Jen Devonshire
Website: www.jendevonshire.co.uk

"Don't overlook the power of well–executed presentation. Put time and effort into figuring out the best way to document your projects — that's a good skill to showcase, too. In portfolios, presentation is key. Badly photographed and pixelated images are an immediate kill."

Lotta Nieminen

Organizing your portfolio

Where possible, tell the story of each project with a narrative that illustrates your approach, considerations and reasoning. Make sure you reference the brief, what you hoped to achieve and the impact that your work had. Create an order that you are comfortable with (this could be chronological, or by project type, personal goals, personal estimations of standard, etc.) but start and end with a couple of pieces that you feel are your best work. Don't be afraid of seeking feedback from friends, teachers or industry professionals. You may also find it helpful to tailor your portfolio to each client, ensuring it is relevant to their business, and/or the work you are bidding for.

In terms of specific spreads, you may choose to display complementary projects, or if you wish to show a range, these may be vastly different in terms of skills and context.

You do want the focus to be on newer work, so perhaps keep this towards the start. A few older pieces later on can show growth and variety though so don't discount these entirely.

Every few months (if not sooner) you should re-evaluate your portfolio, consider the relevance of the work contained and plug any gaps.

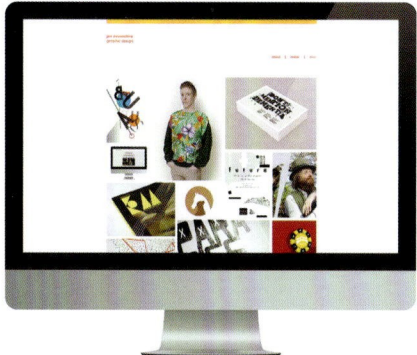

3.19

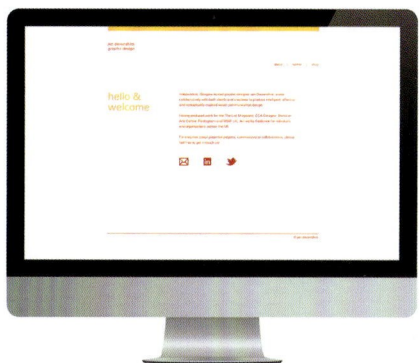

3.20

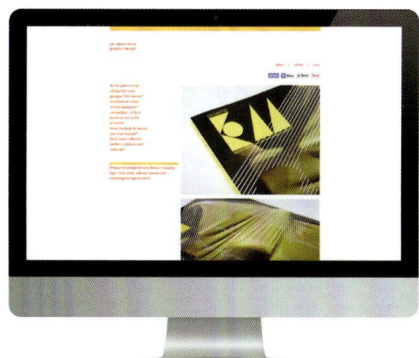

3.21

3.22 — 3.23

Every detail in Lisa Neureiter's personal branding and print portfolio offers information about her: the wooden cover stands for her love of nature, the coptic binding represents Lisa's passion for doing things manually and the transparent pages show her flexibility. A set of postcards are included in the hope they motivate people to write more by hand to celebrate non–digital communication.

Designer: Lisa Neureiter

Website: www.lisaneureiter.com

QUILACHILES | FOOD TRUCK CHILAQUILES

Aimed at young people with focus on authentic Mexican flavour.

CLIENT:
Iteso/Personal Project

FIELDS:
Branding

DATE:
Summer 2014

Top tips: What should be in my physical portfolio?

Pick the strongest work for the front and end of the portfolio.

Be ruthless in your editing and take out anything you don't feel 100% proud of.

Ensure your portfolio includes examples from all aspects of your work and skills — make a list and tick them off.

Include inspiration, preliminary work or work—in—progress imagery and text. For many employers, these are the most important parts of your portfolio, as it shows your ability to translate ideas through into a finished article.

Make sure the work in the portfolio is relevant to the potential employer or client you are meeting.

Don't forget to include inspiration and work—in—progress sketchbooks. You can show them if needed, or leave unopened if not necessary.

Ask the opinion of colleagues, other designers or tutors about your strongest work.

Top tips: How should I present my physical paper portfolio?

Make the presentation easy to transport and carry around, try to limit your portfolio to A3 or smaller.

Invest in a smart portfolio case that you will be proud to carry around.

Choose a portfolio that will allow you to be flexible as to the amount of pages you use and changing the pages is easy to do.

Make sure your portfolio is presented clearly in a way that makes it easy to look through, with uniform paper as 'mounts' or as wrappers to contain groups of un—mounted work, such as drawings.

Present your work in easily identifiable sections, e.g. illustrations or technical spec drawings.

Always include a copy of your résumé in your portfolio.

Always label your portfolio inside with your contact details in case it should be lost or stolen.

www.artsthread.com

Presenting and talking about your portfolio

One rule for presentation that goes across the board is keep it simple, and let the work sing. Build your portfolio so that it truly represents your design abilities, skills and knowledge, and don't let superfluous decoration get in the way.

Your work should speak for itself, but you will be expected to talk through the projects in greater detail at a meeting with a potential employer and offer more detail. The captions that accompany each piece should be short, so this is your chance to offer more and tell the (abridged) story behind the project. Consider:

- What part in the project did you play?

- How did you get the work?

- What were the challenges?

- Did you develop any new skills?

- Are there things you would improve?

- What did you learn from the experience?

When talking through each of the questions, remember to address them in a positive way. You want to make a good impression, and while you need to be realistic, avoid any negative comments (no matter how difficult the client/challenges may have been!).

Whilst you may know your work inside out, can you communicate the essential elements of each project and the thought processes behind them in a few minutes? Practice and edit your pitch so that you have a smooth delivery of the salient points whilst flipping through the pages of your portfolio.

Also, consider what the employer absolutely needs to know. Re-read the job application and make sure you have covered the things they have asked for; use the same terminology and this will make you sound like the obvious choice for the vacancy.

3.24 — 3.26

Lucas Machado wanted to create a printed version of his portfolio that was more than something to present to prospective employers and clients. By designing annual versions of his portfolio he can demonstrate his evolution as a graphic designer.

Designer: Lucas Machado

Website: www.machadolucas.com

3.24

3.25

Considerations: your physical portfolio

There are various technical considerations that should not be overlooked when compiling a portfolio, such as printing work examples on good quality paper and ensuring that they are in good condition and not creased. Try to keep your portfolio compact in A3 (12" x 17" or 29.7cm x 42cm) and pay attention to the quality of the images. If you have photographs that are poorly taken or pixelated, it will signal to the client that you do not show attention to detail, do not care about presentation or lack the technical skills to fix such problems.

Include one image that shows the entire artifact, and back this up with further close–up shots that demonstrate your eye for detail and making skills. When making photographs also consider the background and the environment that you take them in. Some objects work well against a white, while others look better in context (especially if you are looking to demonstrate usage).

If you struggle with photography, ask a photographer to take some shots for you. If you are a recent graduate and don't have a lot of spare cash, then talk to other recent graduates who need experience, or barter your services: photographers need an identity, business card and website etc.

Captions

Each work example should have a caption, which should be minimal and state the title, name of client and overview of the context and skills used. A few short, snappy sentences about your ideas and the thinking behind the project should be included, but don't write a novel. Check your spelling and grammar as mistakes show a lack of attention to detail and can distract from your work.

3.26

Your showreel

If you work regularly with video or animation then a showreel will be essential. Developing a presence on Vimeo, YouTube or similar services can open up a wide audience and provide useful tools to accompany your résumé and portfolio. Vimeo and YouTube are also very shareable tools and if the tone is right, bloggers may look to link to or embed your video in their posts.

Video can be a really useful tool when job–hunting as it allows you to show more of any given project than a flat printed layout can, and this is not limited to video projects. You could show short clips of objects you have designed in use such as books being flicked through or packaging being opened. A traditional print portfolio is great for showing the design of a piece, but not useful when you want to show the experience of using it, which is where video excels. Talking heads can be used to show reactions to your projects. If a particular piece is successful you might consider conducting short interviews with the client, or better still, the users and audience.

A showreel should be relatively short and needs to include clear links to where more information can be found. Much like a print portfolio, showreels are best kept simple and gimmick free. An uncluttered short with a focus on the work will sell you at your best.

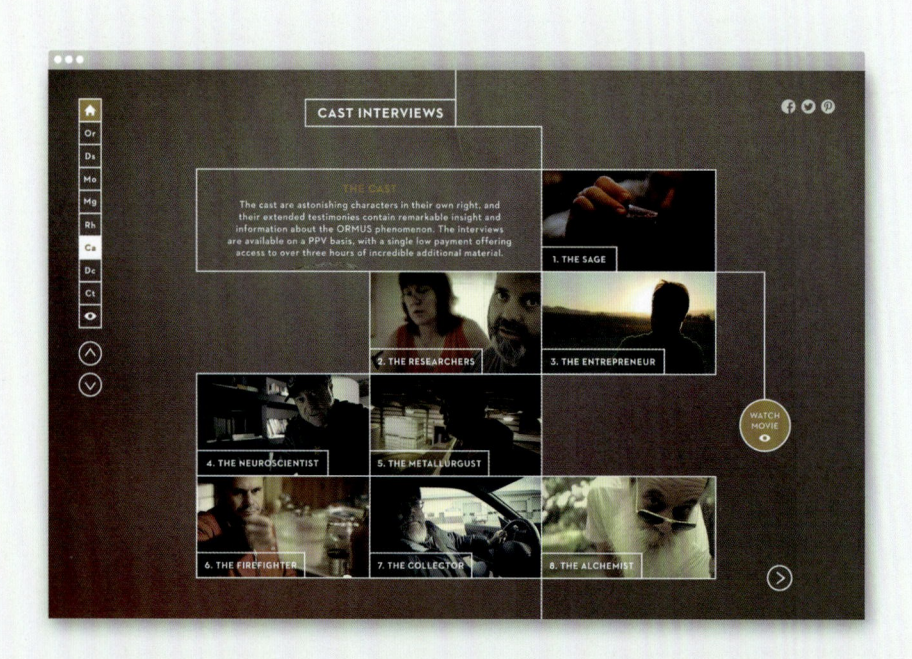

3.27

3.27 + 3.28

Motion graphics is fast becoming a staple in many graphic design portfolios, and this is an area in which Planning Unit excel.

Planning Unit designed the website, poster and onscreen graphics for a fascinating documentary called *All The Gold You Can Eat*, a documentary by filmmaker Joe De Kadt that sets out to explore and unravel one of history's greatest enigmas: the mysterious and secretive art of transforming base metal into gold.

Studio: Planning Unit

Website: www.planningunit.co.uk

Client: Joe De Kadt

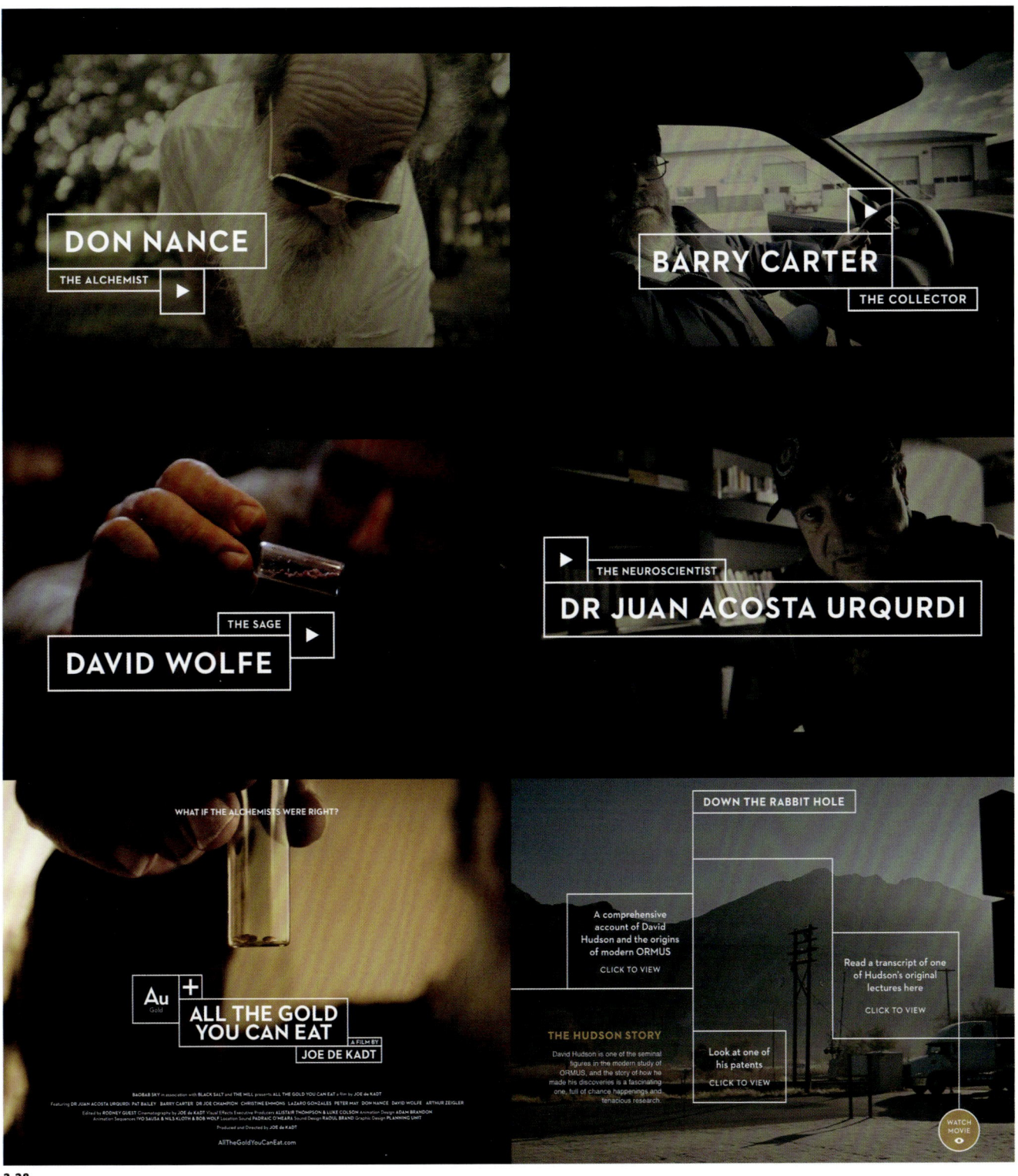

3.28

Networking

Networking, meeting other people engaged or interested in design, is an important skill to cultivate and is necessary if you are to survive as a designer as it shows that you are serious about your career. Networking helps you to develop as a professional by building industry contacts and exchanging or being exposed to new ideas, and ultimately new potential employers and clients. It gives other people in the industry a chance to meet you, learn about you and form an initial impression. When you meet someone new whilst networking you will often hear the magic words "I would like to see that" when you talk about what you are doing. As your career grows and prospers it will become an even more important part of what you do as you seek to meet with potential new clients and grow your business. If you are not going to talk to other people about your abilities and what you can do, business could be very slow, particularly if you are freelancing. Think of it this way: networking provides you with the opportunity to meet new people to pitch to.

Successful people are often also successful networkers. Some people have a talent for it but it is also something that can be learnt and developed with practice. Successful networking means always having a goal. This doesn't have to be too specific, but could be to identify at least two key contacts at design studios you would like to work for or with, or a couple of people who are experts in something that you are deficient in that you will need for an upcoming job. If you go in without any aims, you will almost certainly achieve nothing.

Where do you go to network? If you want to find out about the latest print finishing techniques and new substrates, go to a printing or design event; if you want to meet creatives (designers, artists, illustrators or photographers) go to private showings at galleries, design school shows or other such events where they will be. These events provide a great opportunity to talk shop, learn about new developments and meet people who may be able to help you in the future. You may learn about new techniques for webpage development and creating interactive content, you may meet an expert bookbinder or typographer who could enable you to produce something really unique, or an illustrator who can produce tailor-made images that would shine in your layouts instead of using stock photography. There is no point making new contacts if you don't act on them. This isn't dating, so when you meet someone networking it is normal to drop them an email the next day and use this as a stepping stone to find out more about them, their work or their company, or to continue the discussion you had at the event.

3.29
Glug Serial Cut at Shoreditch Town Hall.
Website: www.glugevents.com
3.30 + 3.31
Glug Brighton.
Website: www.glugevents.com

"Networking isn't asking for a job, but developing connections over beers that may help you land a job in the future."

Cameron Sandage

3.29

3.30

3.31

SPOTLIGHT ON... CAMERON SANDAGE, IBM

Tell us a bit about yourself.

My name is Cameron Sandage, I am a left–handed, one hand clapping, Gemini, multi–disciplined creative currently working as a software designer for IBM in Austin, Texas. Originally from Portland, Oregon I went to school for my bachelors in graphic design with a minor in advertising management at Portland State University. I was trained as a traditional print designer, from running offset presses and screen printing to transitioning in college to be more of a digital designer. But I still do both print and web projects, as well as try to experiment with other mediums.

Could you detail the steps that led to your current career?

Ever since *Toy Story* knew I wanted to do something in the arts, but was not entirely sure what that would be. The school I went to, Reynolds High School in Troutdale, Oregon, had a graphics class with offset presses and screen printing, as well as a commercial arts class. This was where I truly realized what graphic design was and decided that would be my path.

When I graduated from high school in 2005 everyone seemed to want to be a designer. So I teetered back and forth between advertising and graphic design, finally deciding on graphic design and landing a place at Portland State University (PSU) in Portland, Oregon for my bachelor's degree. It was at PSU that I was able to really grow into my career and figure out what I wanted to do. This was mainly due to the professors and the program at the time which was focused on critical thinking. Also being a city university, I was exposed to a lot more of the design work with the AIGA, PAF, AMA, DesignWeek Portland and a slew of other events.

The real steps I took to land where I am today started in my junior year of college when I knew — based on the talent around me both at school and in the Pacific Northwest — that I would need to start looking for a job sooner rather than later. The steps I took were fairly simple: basically, I just started going to various events and networking with people in the industry. This eventually led to an internship with a small digital agency where I worked on my first Nike project. After about 10 months with this agency (internship to junior hire), I wanted to finish up my degree and start looking at possibly moving to a new city.

I went to the AIGA design conference Pivot in Phoenix, Arizona at the beginning of my senior year. Looking back, this was probably the single most significant thing I could have done as a designer still in school. I went along with a box of business cards and ready to expose myself to the larger design community. I met a lot of people (a bunch of whom I still keep in contact with today) from all over the world, but I met one person who would eventually hire me to work at Nike for my first job out of college.

His name was Bjorn Anderson, a Nike design recruiter at the time. I pinged him on Twitter to see if I could meet with him and have him look over my work. I showed him my work on a poorly conceived PDF on my iPad that was half student work, half fake work, and some actual client work from prior agencies or freelance. In the nicest of ways he told me I was not ready for Nike, my book was not solid enough and I needed to do "xyz" if I wanted to work for the swoosh. He then showed me about a half dozen other portfolios of designers on his laptop that he was either actively recruiting or would love to have work at Nike in the future. We talked for about an hour and a half. I left Phoenix with a lot of memories, business cards and greater knowledge about what I needed to do in order to get a real job upon graduating.

A few months later, I was in my senior portfolio class gearing up for my senior show. I had made some 12"x18" glow in the dark posters that said "always working, working always" as a giveaway for the reviewers. After the show was over, I decided to mail a few of these out to people I had met at Pivot, including Bjorn at Nike. Two weeks later he called and asked me if I would be willing to come in for an interview for a three–month contract position with a group called SPARQ. I was excited by the opportunity to interview for a job that might mean I would be both working and going to school for three months as I finished my degree. I went out to Nike and met Bjorn and the hiring manager at SPARQ. A few days later, I was offered the position and started work at Nike as a contract designer with the SPARQ group.

After graduating I was hired full time as a Nike designer for the SPARQ brand and worked for them for almost two years until Nike closed SPARQ and I was laid off. But while at SPARQ I never stopped going to events, meeting people and pushing myself to do things that may have been a little nerve–wracking.

However, I had also stayed in touch with some of the contacts I had made around the country and one told me about the new IBM Design program. I sent them my book, had a phone interview and was flown down to Austin, Texas for an interview. I was hired a few days later and am now a Software Product Designer with IBM living in Austin, Texas.

Please describe your typical day

I don't know if a designer can have a "typical" day or not, my days vary so much depending on the project I am working on or the given task for that week. But I can say that I try to start my day fairly routinely by reading various design blogs — my favorites are *UnderConsideration*, *SwissMiss*, and the *Egotist* in various cities, there are a few others that I will check on occasion as well. Then I'll probably check in with my boss either in person or via email and commence my day. While I was at Nike my day could consist of editing a photo–shoot, mocking up a website, working with a developer, talking out a storyline for a project or working on a variety of other odds and ends.

What's the single best thing about your job?

I think the best thing about being a designer is not knowing what your day will be like or what projects you might be working on. I really like the variety as well as the creative environment as a whole.

What tips would you offer to people who are new to the industry?

If you're still in school, and your professor says design a wine label, don't just do the bare minimum required for the project, make your project different from what others around you are doing. When I was in school I was given a project to design a wine label, instead I (with my project partner) designed a wine beer bottle, with edgy copy and then took high–resolution photos, made the box and turned that in. The professor didn't understand it, but the design world did. I also learned a lot more about the process of selling alcohol and consumers than I would have if I had just made another oval wine label with type and an illustration. Not to say that's a bad way to go, but if there are 10 students in your class all doing the same thing and I am looking to hire a designer out of the 10, I'm probably going to pick the one who pushed the envelope and did something unique versus someone who just did what the professor asked.

Whether you're in school, just graduated or new to the industry, learn to network! Networking is not just handing someone your business card and asking for a job, a great network is made up of people who are in the same industry as you or in related industries. People that you can call as a friend and go grab a beer with. Don't always angle for a job, talk about sports, or the new restaurant that just opened, you don't always have to talk about design. And go to design events, marketing events and any other events that seem of interest which are offered in your city.

SPOTLIGHT ON... NICK CLEMENT, GLUG

Tell us about yourself.

I'm Nick Clement, they say I'm a Creative Director, but I tend just to prefer Designer if we're talking about what I do. I'm Welsh and recently became a dad for the first time. I have a few side projects such as Glug which is presently a monthly gathering of impeccable creative minds, makers and doers that is open to the public in a few countries worldwide and growing quickly,

What advice would you offer to a recent graduate or someone looking to move into the design industry?

Have a good think about what you want to do. Do you want to change the world quickly or make an impact slowly? If quickly, then design might not be for you.

I'd say, as soon as you start your education please realize this isn't enough. Listen and learn, and learn to think. Suck up every form of communication from film to languages and read the business pages. That's going to pay off dividends with future briefs. Learn to sketch and draw, however badly you do it. Listen to people and talk to them, travel, make music, paint, tinker, potter, solder; the design skills will come mainly during or after your course but be ready to come up with problem–solving ideas. Take criticism and be able to give it with grace. Love your surroundings and however

familiar they get try and look at them in other ways, or just get out and have some experiences. This will all feed back into your work and yourself as a vessel.

You're involved in quite a few different organizations. Firstly, how do you find the time, and secondly, do you find one benefits the others?

I don't really find the time, I make the time. I always feel like I'm missing out on something, I guess it keeps me nosy.

Glug is a really interesting concept. What was your motivation for starting this and how do you see it developing?

I'm glad you think it's interesting. It started off as a few tipsy chums from many different agencies talking shop in a pub and has grown to something that Ian (Glug Co–founder) and I are quite proud of. At its core it's a creative "Notworking™" night that celebrates design and creativity from all around the UK but is now spreading to Europe, Asia, the USA and New Zealand. We've a great team of people who give their time for free to the non–profit and help put on these events. We've got some amazing stuff lined up, check the website and please come and be part of it. We do it for the Gluggers.

3.32

3.33

3.34

3.35

3.36

I hope it will grow to become maybe a trade union of creatives; a powerhouse, I think that's got potential for change. We're hoping to do more around education and industry giving back. But in the meantime we've got a few things planned that we hope to launch soon.

You've had a varied career and faced lots of exciting creative challenges. How do you prepare when you are looking to enter not just a new job, but also an entirely different sector?

Well, it's been mainly digital since the early 2000s but we're all winging it a little I guess. Do your research, embrace change and as a freelance I've met some incredible people along the way. There's been many an eye opening moment.

What has been the key to your career progression?

Resilience, a good network, being honest and not afraid of new challenges, the ability to take the regular wobbles, knocks and occasional failures combined with a little bit of knowing something about a lot of things I guess.

Networking is often more challenging to young designers than producing work. Are there any tips you could offer people looking to access new clients and opportunities?

It's all about your network and keeping working at it. I think Mr Anthony Burrill summed it up pretty well with "Work hard & be nice to people".

3.32 + 3.33
Glug Brighton.
Website: www.glugevents.com
3.34 — 3.36
Wolff Olins Glug at Cargo.
Website: www.glugevents.com

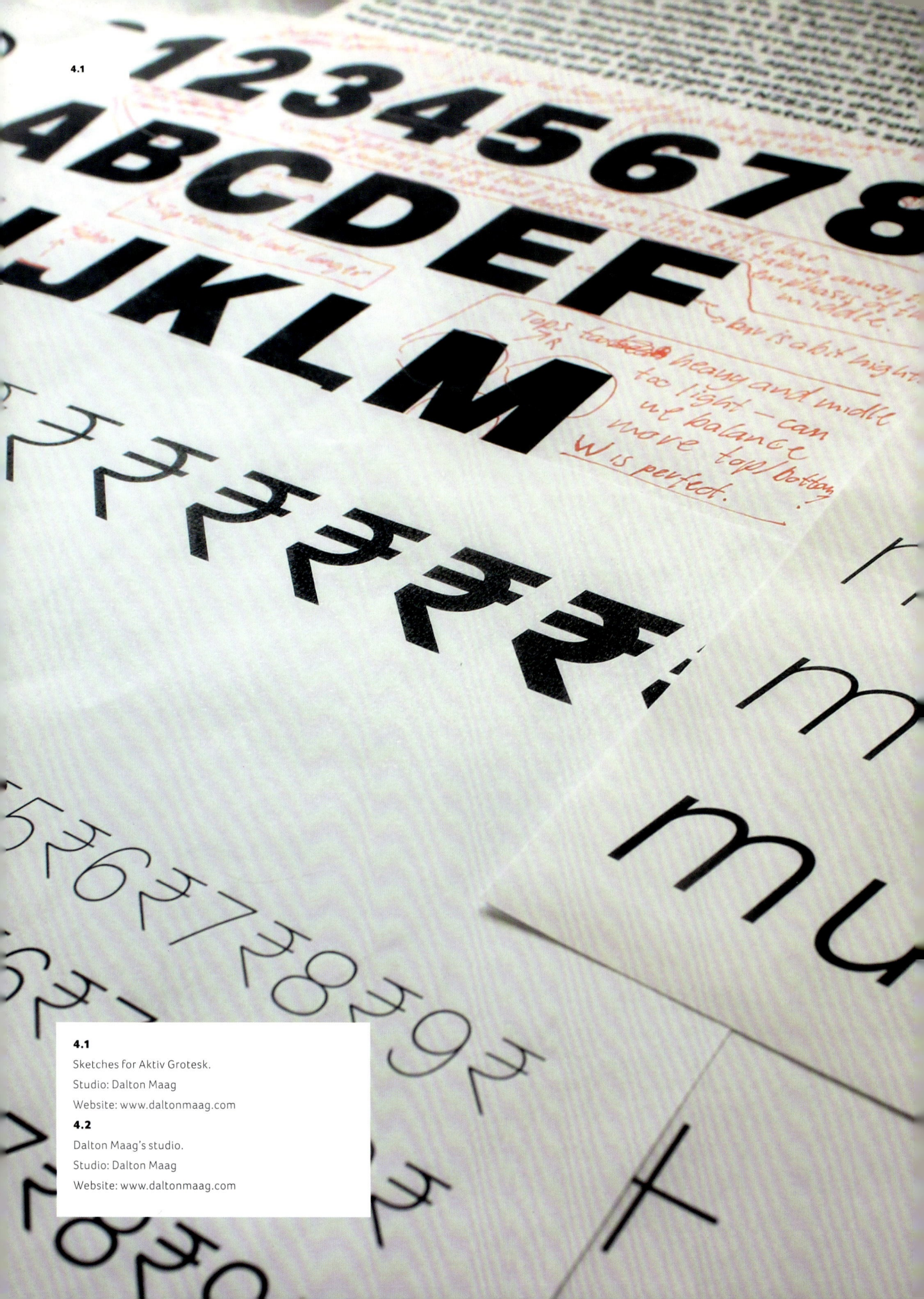

4.1
Sketches for Aktiv Grotesk.
Studio: Dalton Maag
Website: www.daltonmaag.com
4.2
Dalton Maag's studio.
Studio: Dalton Maag
Website: www.daltonmaag.com

CHAPTER 4
GETTING A JOB

In terms of employment, the opportunities within the design industry are numerous. To find what may be some of the best opportunities you should look at where the industry is going and where it is developing as this is probably where there will be skills shortages, the highest paid jobs, and the most interesting and challenging briefs. In this chapter, we will look more closely at the numerous opportunities available to graphic design graduates.

4.2

In this chapter we will:

- *Examine various sectors of the design industry.*
- *Discuss the job hunting process and methods for making it easier.*
- *Suggest ways for putting together a good résumé.*
- *Suggest ways to get through the interview process.*

Choosing the right direction

To make the right choice, first look at what you enjoyed the most and then where your skills lie. If these two answers are the same, then you've probably made your choice. Use the SWOT matrix in Chapter 3 to help you focus. For example, if you enjoy web design and have a good knowledge of the relevant software and skills, then you should start looking for web design jobs. If you enjoy a particular area, but lack some of the necessary skills, don't despair: there can be opportunities to enter industry at a beginner level, perhaps as an intern, with an agency that is willing to train you. Many design studios prefer to recruit people who they can train in their way of approaching design problems.

The work available will also depend on where you are living and how flexible you are about that. Most cities have universities or colleges that produce new design graduates every year who will apply for a limited number of jobs. If you are willing to consider moving to a different city, you may increase your chances of finding a job. Whatever your skills and interests, there are jobs available, but like all jobs, it takes perseverance and hard work to find the one that is right for you. Be sure to self-promote and network to carve out opportunities for yourself and differentiate yourself from all the other recent graduates also looking to take their first step on the career ladder.

If you do find that employers are looking for some skills that you do not have or that you are weak in, do something about it. Most cities have a range of courses available in their educational institutions and there are web tutorials available for most things now. Put the hours in and practice to fill any gaps in your résumé.

A job with a design studio or web design agency may be the most coveted positions, but you can also broaden your search to other companies: most businesses use and therefore need design skills in one way or another. Real estate agents, for example, or grocery retailers, depend on their web pages or brochures to generate sales and these need to be designed to be attractive, current and to attract potential buyers.

Increasingly, coffee shops, bars and restaurants, and in fact most small businesses, have a website to let people know about what they do and the specialist services they provide. Look at what businesses are near to where you live and look at how they present themselves. While there may not be opportunities for full-time employment, you may find opportunities to do freelance work that will add current commercial projects to your portfolio.

4.3

4.4

NEW WRITING MATTER 13

WAY OUT

thing which might be
yet dead, is that, mar
and been unable to p
little table attached t
Processing Room Fa
size for your eye sigh

God has never …

• Made good use of the concepts of good and evil
• Delivered punishment or reward in or after life
• Controlled any organism or inanimate object
• Made anything with a real purpose or plan
• Needed to be worshipped
• Expected anything of you
• Been accurately conceived of

After God knows how long - and as you might have
gathered from the leaflet, God doesn't know how long
- you recognise a name being called as your own. You
automatically stand. All at once you become acutely
aware of who you were and every memory you ever had.
An overwhelming tangle of sensations, notions, thoughts
and experiences flow through you and out beyond the
Way Out door. The only thing you process as you follow,
is the contents of the public information leaflet left
behind on your warm seat.

Well you did ask.

20   21

4.3 — 4.6

Fruitful and successful partnerships can
come from making good local contacts;
these are often the clients that come back
for more. This is the 8th edition of *Matter*
(a bespoke publication created for the MA
Creative Writing students at Sheffield Hallam
University), designed and illustrated by
Sheffield based Eleven Design.

Studio: Eleven Design

Website: www.elevendesign.co.uk

Client: Sheffield Hallam University

Design for print

Print is a huge business. No matter what developments come along in terms of web and digital technologies, there will always be a call for print, and with digital publishing there is an ever-increasing overlap between these areas. The digital revolution has removed many of the intermediary printing trades rather than the need or desire to print. Print design is generally very fast paced with tight deadlines, so expect late nights and tense moments when projects finally go to print. Print design is particularly attractive to graduates because it allows you to work with both text and image, and end up with a beautifully printed artifact that will look great in your portfolio. It is also perhaps the area that is closest to much of the material you studied and worked on throughout your design course.

Design for print is used by a wide range of sectors, from book and magazine publishing, to advertising, the creation of posters, stationery, brochures and catalogs. Within print design, you may work in any number of roles, from layout design, cover design, illustration and general art working. Content checking, editing and copywriting may also be part of the designer's palette. Working in print design will really sharpen your abilities in specific areas. When working in print, the level of attention to detail required cannot be understated as print projects are a big investment for a client and the design studio as the design firm will normally pay for printing and invoice the client later. You absolutely have to get things right, or else you may be faced with the bill for a reprint.

Work on bespoke items such as business cards and personal stationery allows you to work with high-quality print and finishing processes to generate really attractive items. All businesses want their stationery to stand out, and a clever, well-considered design with a spot varnish or a well-placed die cut can achieve this.

Working with typography is another benefit of designing for print. Bespoke lettering and type for identities, promotional material and magazine design, can become a career in itself, especially if you take great enjoyment in creating your own typefaces.

Promotional print design is one area where there will always be work; no matter how successful online digital technologies are, businesses will always look to produce banners, catalogs and flyers as direct ways of reaching their audience. Direct mail and other marketing and promotional literature are a source of regular income for many design studios, and while the work may not be glamorous, it pays the bills. And once in a while a client may require something special that enables the designer to be much more creative, such as when producing an invite that really stands out.

Within print design, the technology and processes don't change at the same rate as for online tools, but this does not mean it is a static industry. There are trends, developments and new ways of working that you will need to keep up with, and you will need to possess a deep knowledge of the software that are industry standard for print work such as InDesign, Photoshop and Illustrator. To work in print, you will need more than a good understanding of typography and layout: there are a number of technical processes you will need to be familiar with, such as producing the color separations that will be sent to the printers. You will need a good knowledge of the entire printing process including print finishing, from binding methods to die cuts, the use of special colors/inks to having an understanding of paper stock itself. By learning and understanding how the printer and print finisher do their part of the process, you will be able to take their requirements into account when you design something, making you better equipped to do commercial work and avoiding costly mistakes. A good printer will always be able to advise you about the technical possibilities and limitations of different processes, and advancements that will make your working life a lot easier.

> *"When working in print, if you are unsure about anything (color, bleed, folding, die cuts, anything about how to build your file), call the printer. Tell them you're a brand new designer and you'd like their help building a good file. They'll be delighted you asked instead of sending them a messy file."*
>
> **Monet Fort, Senior Graphic Designer, Professional Education at Georgia Institute of Technology**

4.7 — 4.9

Living the Nordic Light — a tribute to the 100 year olds of the North, captured forever in this bespoke print–based artifact.

By interviewing four people over 100 years old who have lived their entire lives above the Arctic Circle, Snøhetta explores the effect of living in, and in the absence of, Nordic Light.

People born in the beginning of the last century are the last living generation to have experienced changes that have had a tremendous physical impact on humanity in the western world. They witnessed two world wars, worldwide changes in transportation, power supply transitions, revolutions, industrialization and the overwhelming introduction of the digital era. With *Living the Nordic Light*, Snøhetta aimed to capture individual experiences related to the indisputable presence of light, shade, and darkness, before and after the introduction of electricity.

Studio: Snøhetta

Website: www.snohetta.com

Client: Zumtobel Group

4.7

4.8

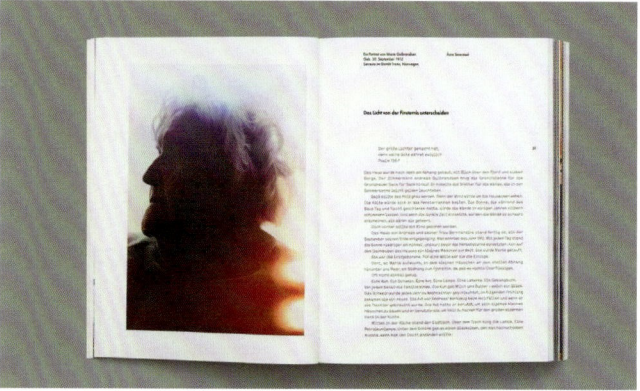

4.9

ANSVARIG
UTGIVARE
Peter Hjelm

TRYCK &
DISTRIBUTION
DanagårdLiTHO

JOURNALISTER
Cecilia Campell
Magnus Ekbladh

REDAKTION &
GRAFISK DESIGN
Snask

FOTOGRAFI &
ILLUSTRATION
Snask

Nygammalt
Old Is The New New

"Det var bättre förr" är ett påstående man inte ofta hör. Det är ju, förstås, ytterst sällan det stämmer. Men visst är det lätt att bli nostalgisk och att med blida ögon se tillbaka på den tid som flytt. Tanken om att det var bättre förr slog säkert även Johannes Gutenberg, då han på 1450-talet satt i sin verkstad i Mainz i västra Tyskland och utvecklade den europeiska boktryckarkonsten (helt ovetande om att man vid den tiden i Kina tryckt böcker på papper i minst 1000 år). Men frågan är om han skulle tycka det var så vansinnigt mycket bättre förr ifall han mirakulöst återuppstått och fått se vad hans tankar och uppfinningar lett till i dagens moderna tryckkonst. Till exempel är hans främsta verk den så kallade Mazarinbibeln, som han med sin nya teknik hann trycka upp 180 exemplar av på tre år. Bra tempo, med tanke på att det tidigare tagit tre år att färdigställa ett enda exemplar. Hantverk i all ära, men kanske skulle han ändå snabbt överge nostalgin om han fick reda på att vi idag skulle kunna trycka 1000-tals biblar om dagen, kompletta med omslag och limbundna.

Vad vi däremot kan vara säkra på är att det gäller att hänga med i utvecklingen. Att sträva efter att göra "som man alltid gjort" får aldrig bli ett självändamål. Däremot finns det ju ett stort värde i att vara stolt över sitt arv och att hela tiden försöka bli bättre på det man gör – en mentalitet vi på DanagårdLiTHO alltid utgått från.

Då vårt förra nummer av Printing Friends handlade om det allra senaste har vi alltså som motpol valt att i det här numret ta en promenad längs minnenas allé, ända tillbaka till Gutenbergs tid. Vi berättar om DanagårdLiTHOs rötter, om dagstidningarnas ovilja att förändra sig på 70-talet och så har vi träffat branschräven och typografen Gideon Beil som berättar om sin 45-åriga karriär inom tryckarbranschen. Missa heller inte att kolla in vårt showroom med ett urval av våra senaste stiliga trycksaker. Trevlig höstläsning!

Peter Hjelm: Vd DanagårdLitho

4.10

In 2010, Danagård and LiTHO merged to create DanagårdLiTHO, an exciting Swedish printing company with over 100 employees. Directly after merging, they realized that their #1 customer touch point, the journal *Printing Friends*, was uninspiring and totally lacked design; a shameful insight, coming from a printing company.
To bring about change, Snask was asked to conceive a total re−make and to develop the product to sync with brand goals and vision.

In the beginning of the process Snask realized that DanagårdLiTHO needed to do more than just polish the graphic style of the magazine. Snask developed a strategy around inspiring art directors and graphic designers by making a customer magazine that looked better than their own agencies' printed matter. If art directors and graphic designers got inspired it would surely inspire everyone else with less of an eye for print design. When putting the magazine together, Snask was in charge of the whole shebang: conceptualization, content, design, illustration, journalism and photography.

Studio: Snask

Website: www.snask.com

Client: DanagårdLiTHO

Branding

Branding is so much more than a logo.

Branding is a concept that shapes how a product or service is produced or provided and design is a key factor in building a brand. A company or product has a combination of attractive characteristics such as quality, durability, value, quick performance and so on. It may be very good at what it does, be sincere and reliable, but that is not enough to create a successful brand. Brand building requires the adequate and appropriate communication of these special characteristics so that other people start to believe that the brand has them as well.

A brand is built over an extended period of time, through the repetition of the brand message and the confirmation of this by people's experience using the products or dealing with the organization. The one constant in brand building is the need to communicate, and every communication should reinforce and complement the brand message and what it stands for.

Assuming that the brand characteristics are desirable to the target group, the design of brand communication will be at the heart of its success or failure. The choice of words and images and how they are presented — the font, the weight, the tone — can dramatically change how a brand is perceived and received. Branders often do testing with focus groups to see how potential end-users respond to different images, colors or strap lines, and then hone the brand communication based on the results generated.

Communications design and branding is often something that is thought of as happening towards the end of a project, as part of the implementation of a product launch, for example. As design studios migrate from being service providers towards becoming strategic partners of their clients, they are increasingly challenging this traditional approach and insisting on becoming themselves an integral part of the product, brand or service creation. Designers are thus increasingly having an influence that goes beyond creating the public face of a company or product.

To create an effective brand you will need to fully understand the company you are working for inside out; you will need to understand where they are from, where they are heading, who their client base is, and what business they want to attract. In essence, you need to have clearly understood the particular niche the company inhabits, the qualities it has and how it wishes to grow. A client won't come to a branding company or designer if they are happy with their business; they will come to you when they are looking to fix something or achieve something greater such as reaching a new audience or moving into new markets.

Brand design work ranges from brand tweaks to complete overhauls that will take a brand in a new direction. Rarely will a designer have the opportunity to start building a brand from scratch.

4.11 — 4.13

Branding for Nasty Gal, an international fashion retailer offering new and vintage clothing; photographs taken in their Los Angeles headquarters.

Designer: Emily Hadden

Website: www.emilyhadden.com

Client: Nasty Gal

4.11

4.12

Advertising and marketing

The world of advertising and marketing can be an extremely fast paced and exciting place to work in, creating the visual communications that aim to reach the hearts, minds and wallets of particular target groups. While the ultimate goal may be selling, advertising and marketing design encompasses a range of processes and collaborations that inform the design process, such as market research, conducting focus groups to discuss the effectiveness of packaging design or messaging, and working with other specialists like photographers, copywriters, social media gurus and web designers.

Some clients will be open to the use of highly creative solutions and have budgets available to facilitate this, trusting in you to create innovative work that will be noticed, particularly when there is a new product launch or rebrand. But they will also be very demanding and exacting, expecting

nothing short of perfection. A good, well-executed campaign will get you noticed and help you gain exposure, which is key to winning bigger clients with larger budgets.

Larger companies tend (but not always) to work with larger design studios that have the range and quantity of personnel that are able to handle big jobs. All organizations need advertising and marketing however, and not all can afford the fees of large agencies and so there is ample space for freelancers in advertising and marketing design.

The work produced will normally be presented and accessed across multiple platforms including television, web, print and even physical artifacts. As a designer, you'll need to have a good overview of current trends and technologies in order to make sure your outcomes reach the maximum potential audience.

4.14 + 4.15

The first initiative campaign from Partners for Mental Health designed to improve mental health in Canada. Critical to its success was to create an experience that would draw people into a conversation, encourage a new, more open relationship with their feelings, and inspire them to pledge their support. The identity thus had to be bold yet personal and comfortable. To do this, Blok Design created a spectrum of moods and corresponding colors that people could identify with, select and wear. They then put it out on the street to provoke engagement and dialog, driving people to the website where they could learn more and pledge their support.

Studio: Blok Design

Website: www.blokdesign.com

Client: Partners in Mental Health

4.14

4.15

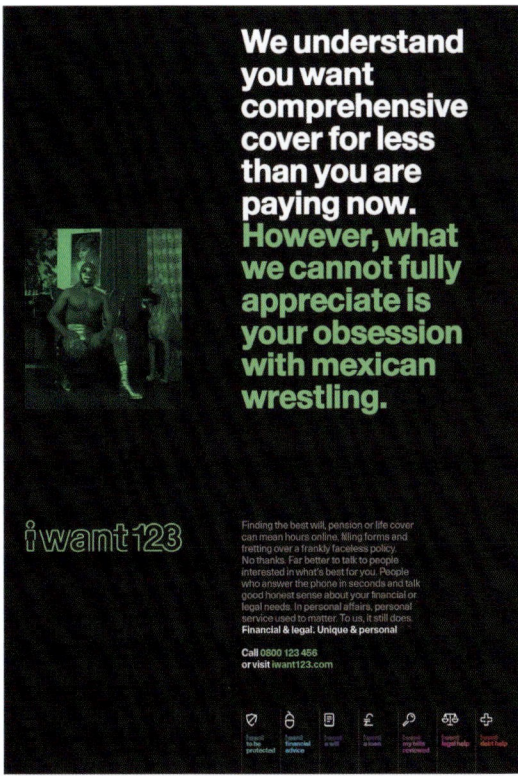

4.16

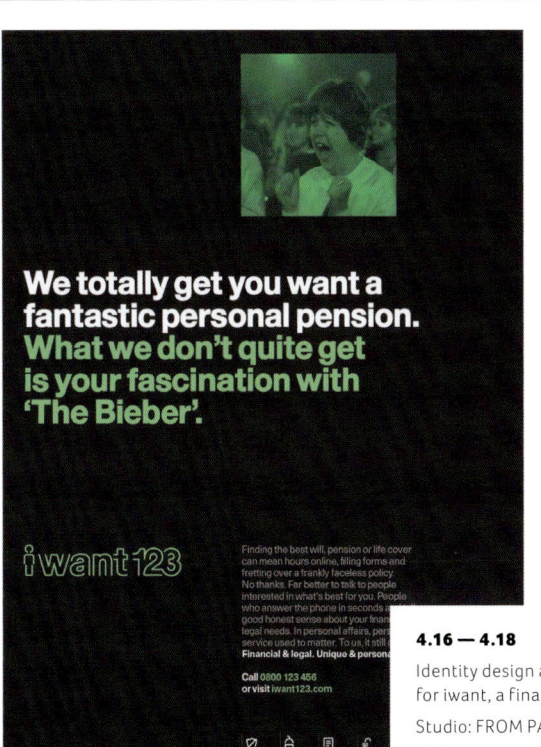

4.17

4.16 — 4.18

Identity design and advertising collateral for iwant, a financial concierge service.

Studio: FROM PARTS UNKNOWN

Website: www.frompartsunknown.co.uk

Client: iwant

4.18

Website design and apps

Web design is a wonderful industry to work in as the technology is constantly evolving and there are always new avenues to explore. The web is still relatively young when compared to the long history of print. We tend to forget that Tim Berners-Lee developed HTML in 1989.

Comparatively, Apps are a relatively recent innovation — the technology is still developing as the capabilities of mobile and tablet devices grow. Unlike many websites, apps often draw on the device to create and present content — you can program the app to respond to GPS data, or take images or video direct from the camera and then manipulate and share the results.

There are many jobs associated with web and app design and you don't have to be a coder to be part of this industry, although having coding skills is a definite advantage. Websites and apps all require imagery, copy and design to communicate effectively and this is the core business of a graphic designer.

Designers can create the design template for a website and either code it themselves or pass it on to a coder to do so. In essence, this is similar to the way that print processes used to work as a designer marked up a document and a typesetter would then layout the page. With the web, the design, content and coding are

similarly separate; HTML (or database) holds the content while CSS and tools like JQuery take care of the look, feel and functionality.

This division means that there are specific areas in which you can specialize and it is not expected that you will be able to do everything yourself. As the range of web technologies develop and grow, it becomes increasingly unlikely that a designer will be able to do everything, and your role will perhaps be more that of a project manager that harnesses the work of other professionals.

> *"Being a graphic designer is awesome and all, but as jobs in printed medium are getting scarcer, things are moving to digital/online mediums, that is where things are headed and what employers and potential clients are looking for. If you learn the workings behind websites/programs etc., you will get ahead and be more versatile.*
>
> *There is certainly a lot of creativity to be had in website design these days and you can do so much with the look and feel of a web page/mobile site/ app. Good places to learn include Codecademy and Treehouse."*
>
> **Michelle Dinan, designer and front-end dev, michelledinan.com**

> *"Learn to code. You need technical web design skills to be competitive."*
>
> **Monet Fort, Senior Graphic Designer, Professional Education at Georgia Institute of Technology**

4.19 — 4.21

Interface design for Beautified, an app that helps find and book last-minute beauty appointments from a curated group of top-tier salons and spas.

Designer: Lotta Nieminen

Website: www.lottanieminen.com

Client: Beautified

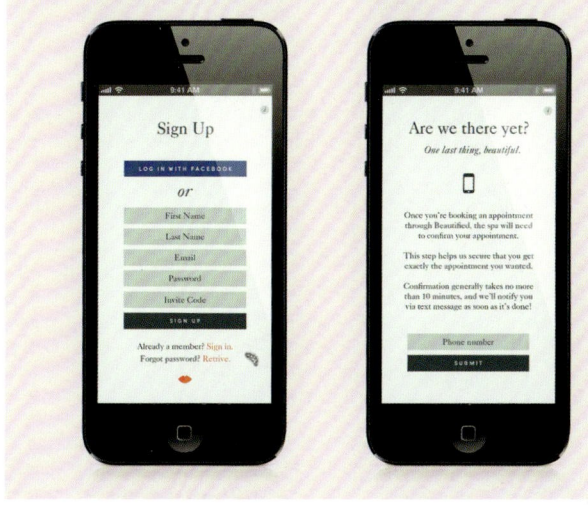

4.19

4.20

4.21

Motion graphics and animation

Not all graphic design projects are flat and printed. Some design solutions will require non-linear structure and presentation of the web. As the number and power of digital devices that people use grows, content generators are pushing the boundaries of what content they deliver and how they deliver it. From chat and photo sharing applications to streaming of films and real-time content, a designer has to pull together and incorporate many different information sources. This is the current leading edge of a long-standing relationship between the disciplines of film, animation and graphic design.

The clear historical links between print and television advertising show that graphic design has been engaged with motion graphics for decades. The film industry increasingly hires design specialists to produce stunning title sequences such as those to *Casino Royal* (2006). See www.artofthetitle.com for more examples.

The power of animation is its ability to break free of reality and express ideas and concepts in ways that film cannot. If you want a talking cat, you can invest heavily in CGI, try to train a cat and voiceover it, or work with an animator. By using animation you are not confined to what can be filmed easily, only by what you can imagine. Animation excels in instructional pieces where you want a message to be clear, focusing on specific things without unnecessary distractions, such as the safety sequences shown on airplanes before takeoff.

Today, designers need to consider how a design can translate into and successfully harness various motion graphics tools across multiple platforms. Websites are increasingly showing rather than telling, replacing text with animations and films that show off a product or concept, and these are becoming increasingly interactive.

Despite all the bells and whistles that can now be incorporated into a website or other digital project, design principles remain valid: each piece of content must serve a function and add to the overall design rather than being incorporated just because they can be. For a budding graphic designer, the use of some motion graphics can help add a zing to your online portfolio and make it interactive.

4.22 — 4.24

Intimacy production stills. This was five friends' submission to CTN's 6th annual 24 hour animation contest, co-created by Andrew Selveraj, Audrey Aquino, Carlos Enciso, Dakota Hopkins and Jason Beale. The contest was to create a 30-second animation around the theme "What if you only had 24 hours to live."

Team: Jason Beale, Audrey Aquino, Dakota Hopkins, Carlos Enciso & Andrew Selvaraj

Websites:
www.JasonBeale.me
www.audreyaquino.com
www.dakotahopkins.com
www.carlosenciso.com
www.kreap.allyou.net

Winner: Student Silver ADDY Winner in Non-Traditional Advertising, AAF 2014

4.22

4.23

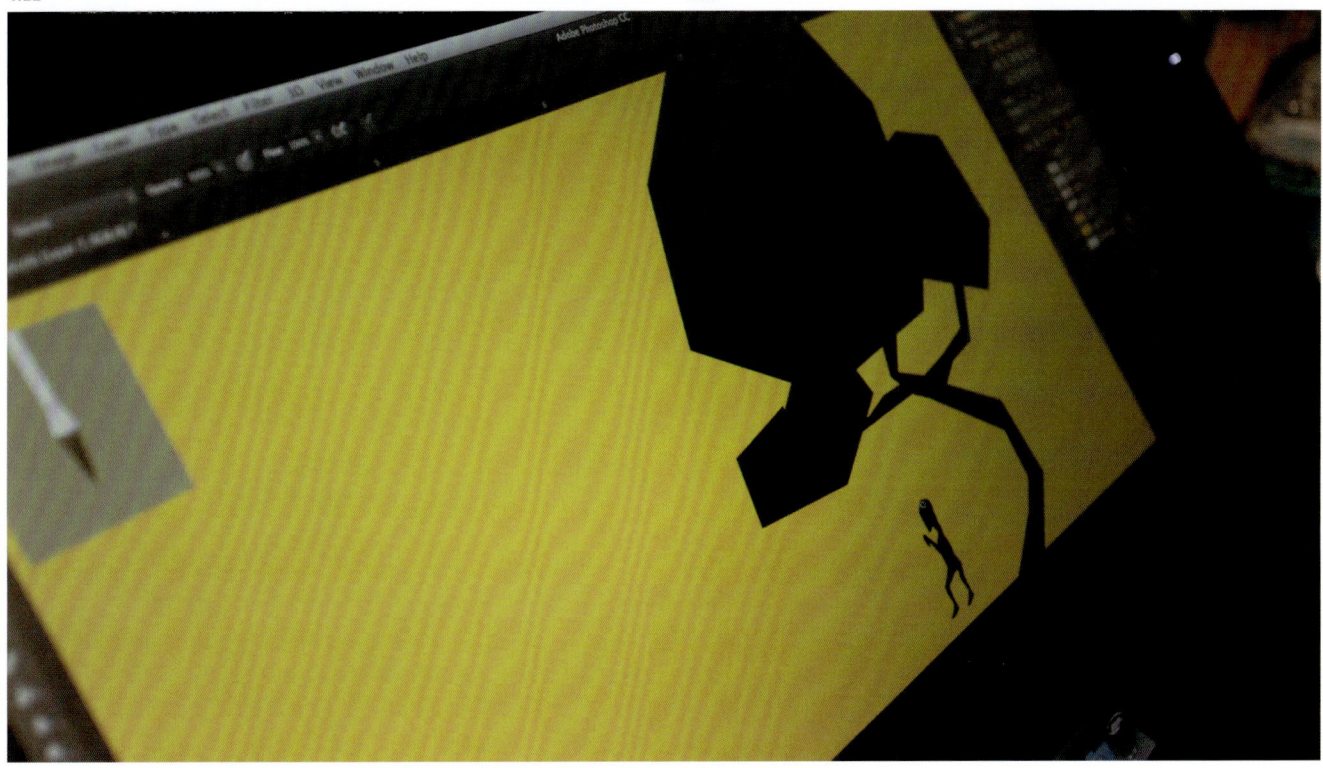

4.24

4.25

4.26

4.27

Moving image

Some iconic practitioners, such as Saul Bass and Kyle Cooper, have had careers that have bridged that gap between moving image and graphic design. While it is rare for a designer to work exclusively with moving image, it is an essential part of cross–channel campaigns, so an understanding of the language of film is essential. Graphic designers are involved in the production of motion pictures by creating the title sequences and peripheral areas like the design of props, and they also work with moving image to produce advertisements, blips, idents, instructional videos and more. Much of this is advertising and promotional work that was previously limited to television. Television advertising is still the standard for many companies and campaigns because it works: you can talk to people directly in their homes, and if the message is memorable, it will stick. Video and animation sequences are increasingly used in websites, applications and other interactive areas because they can tell a story in a way that static media such as print can't. Even a few short frames can engage, entertain and inform, which is why it is such a useful tool.

Any design project that utilizes moving image can be costly and there are many more factors to be considered than for a standard design project. When budgeting for this type of work, you may need to consider the costs of actors, animators, studios, locations, editing, script writers, director, cameramen and the specialist equipment that will be required during production. In addition to motion and time factors, audio will add another dimension to a project. A few well–chosen words or pieces of music can connect to people on a very personal and emotional level.

Thankfully much of this can be achieved with very affordable design software and equipment. Digital cameras have evolved to the point that you can capture high–resolution footage at a very low cost, and animation development has become more rapid due to technological developments. Many productions have been created using non–specialist tools, cheap cameras (with good lenses!) and basic editing suites. Doing something cheaply doesn't mean cutting corners.

"Normally clients don't know all too much about the production of film. When it comes to live action sets, invite your clients. It's something that feels obvious but many forget this or think it's better to not have the client on set. But a few hours won't hurt. The client will really appreciate it. Get away from the desk and boring office as well as seeing you work and get inspired by your professional on set profession. When cutting the film get your client to swing by when you edit the film and let them see what's going on. Don't do this too much or you'll end up with trouble. But keep them in the loop and make them feel like they are a part of the production."

Fredrik Öst snask.com

4.25 — 4.27

Stills from *Intimacy*. The project was fully realized from concept to animation in just one day.

Team: Jason Beale, Audrey Aquino, Dakota Hopkins, Carlos Enciso & Andrew Selvaraj

Websites:
www.JasonBeale.me
www.audreyaquino.com
www.dakotahopkins.com
www.carlosenciso.com
www.kreap.allyou.net

Winner: Student Silver ADDY Winner in Non–Traditional Advertising, AAF 2014

SPOTLIGHT ON… JANINE VAGOOL (*UPPERCASE* MAGAZINE)

Tell us a bit about yourself.

I'm the publisher, editor and designer of UPPERCASE publishing inc — I publish *UPPERCASE*, a quarterly print magazine for the creative and curious as well as books on illustration, craft and creativity.

My first job following graduation from art college was working for a design firm specializing in signage and wayfinding. I spent months setting up signage files for production (i.e. specifying the position and design of the washroom signs in the local sports arena). Needless to say, it wasn't very inspiring. My boss was also sexist and would refer to me as "little girl". Every time I corrected him, I got a raise. I doubled my salary by the time I quit, about nine months later.

Working in that first job was excellent motivation to become my own boss. I developed my design style and roster of clients over the next few years, specializing in print design for arts and culture clients. I did everything from small ads to large publications and marketing materials, as well as publication design for books and art publications.

How did *UPPERCASE* begin, and what were the key inspirations/drivers?

Following the closure of an independent magazine that I freelanced for, the "magazine" section of my brain was free to explore. I had fantasized about designing my own magazine and I was getting tired of working for clients on their ideas but not my own. It also coincided with the closure of some mainstream magazines (*Domino*, Martha Stewart's *Blueprint*) and I recognized there was a void for a well–designed, visually inspiring publication. The content came from my own interests as a graphic designer, but the magazine is not specifically about graphic design…

The tagline is "for the creative and curious" — this is a broad statement but the content is inspired by design, illustration, typography and craft. I like to find creative tangents for our themes, engage our readership to participate in calls for content and imagery, and we often collaborate directly with our readers on articles.

4.28, 4.30 + 4.31
Spreads of *UPPERCASE* magazine.
Studio: UPPERCASE
Website: www.uppercasemagazine.com
4.29
UPPERCASE magazine proof.
Studio: UPPERCASE
Website: www.uppercasemagazine.com

4.28

4.29

4.30

4.31

How do you source so much wonderful material for *UPPERCASE*?

I'm always looking on blogs, Twitter, Instagram and sites like Etsy, Flickr, Behance and Dribbble for interesting work. But as our readership grows, a lot of the content is finding me through our submissions forms.

UPPERCASE readers inspire me. They are so talented!

In terms of your career path, when and how did you know that you'd made the right choice?

I studied visual communications in college and was always focused on a career in graphic design. Once I worked in the industry for a dozen years, I felt that I wasn't being sufficiently challenged and began to see how I could use my skills in other ways.

From observation over the years that I freelanced, I learned how to plan and market events, how to budget for media, how to edit texts and — most importantly — how to multitask. Through the freelancer's lifestyle, I also learned how to acclimate to the stresses of deadlines and uncertain pay checks. It felt natural that

I use these skills and combine it with my entrepreneurial spirit and start making books and magazines.

***UPPERCASE* magazine has done fantastically well in an age of blogs and social media; while these web–based outlets could be seen as competition, you've used them to help the magazine find its audience. Do you have any tips for designers looking to launch their own projects?**

I don't see digital media such as online magazines, iPad versions and other distractions as competition for *UPPERCASE* magazine. And I have no plans of offering the magazine in any other format than print. People come to us because they love print, they love the handmade and tactile, the do–it–yourself ethos... There's a perception online that the magazine is bigger than it is; in fact it is a solo enterprise (with a roster of great contributors). The Internet doesn't show the full story, often. But that can be a benefit, too. With the Internet and social media it is so much easier for young designers to get noticed. My advice is to be media–savvy... to know how to market yourself to the right people. Don't be afraid to put yourself out there.

Looking for jobs

Most jobs are not advertised in the traditional sense. The cost of taking out an advertisement in a relevant publication for a junior graphic designer is an expense most firms will try and avoid. Instead, many recruit for posts of this type by recommendations, or direct from graduate shows. More senior positions are occasionally advertised (especially management positions), and recruiters may be utilized, but the vast majority of positions are filled through posts on social media (see 136 for more information) or on the company's website.

The best way to find a job in the industry is to be on the inside, so follow the companies you would like to work with on social media, and look out for posts in the "Careers" or "Work with us!" section of their website. If any suitable opportunities come up (perhaps not a job, but freelance work or an internship), then apply or ask for an informal chat. Once your face is known, and your colleagues are aware of your abilities, then it is likely you will be recommended for the job that you really want.

Some larger design companies have talent spotters, and will get out to places where they might uncover the next big thing, so be active! If you show your work in exhibitions, submit projects to magazines and blogs, maintain a good social media presence and talk about design; soon enough the right people will notice you.

When it comes to applying for jobs advertised in newspapers or online, be selective. While the instinct may be to apply for any job going, try to be more targeted and reserve your efforts for the handful of places you would really like to work.

Ask yourself:

- Does the opportunity align with your interests and skills?

- Is there a future in this role and/or room for progression?

- Do they have interesting clients or projects?

- In looking for a job there are a lot of things to consider aside from whether or not you would like to do the work. Think carefully about the geography, pay, hours and chance of progression.

- Deciding which career path you will choose depends on your personality, ambition, skill and many other factors. The biggest decisions will be whether you want to work for yourself or for someone else and the type of work that you want to do.

Online job resources

www.twitter.com
Where design jobs are first advertised.

www.creativeboom.com
Ideas, inspirations, and importantly, jobs.

www.krop.com
Build your portfolio and look for jobs.

www.behance.net/joblist
Portfolios, communities and job listings.

www.designjobs.aiga.org
US graphic design jobs.

www.designobserver.com/jobs/
Articles, jobs and much more.

www.jobs.smashingmagazine.com
An exhaustive list of opportunities.

www.thinkcreatedo.co.uk
Opportunities throughout the UK.

www.linkedin.com
The best place to network online.

www.designweek.co.uk
UK, and international jobs.

"Differentiate yourself. Do more than your job role. Be active, pick up hobbies, have passions. All those you compete against will also be able to fulfil the job requirements, but what can you offer that's different?"

Adpreneurs

Top tips: Researching the job market

Research into depth who you want to work for, and then approach them with that info. Show that you care and prepare well — from first approach all the way to your interview. What is their reputation? What are they known for? What's the culture and values? What work have they done recently? Who are their clients? Have they won any awards? What do you think about their work? What talents have you got that can help them? The more you know about them, the better and more appropriately you can pitch when you approach them, or when you get your interview.

Think about what you can do for your client or future employer, not just what they can do for you. What are your specific talents? And why would that be useful to them in particular? Think about your technical and creative skills, but also about your project management and time management skills, your interests and passions. The more you know about yourself and what's needed in the market place, the more likely it is you will get a job offer.

When applying for jobs it isn't really about the quantity of applications you send, but about the quality. I regularly get emails from people who want to work for us. If they had spend 5 min researching us on the web, then they would know what we do, what my name is (and the correct spelling of it!) and that we are extremely small. I know it is soul destroying when you have been looking for a job for a long time (I have been there!), but you need to show up and show that you care about getting a potential job. Please, never send an email with 'Dear Sirs' as that's one of the quickest ways to end up being deleted.

Many jobs aren't actually advertised. You need to start looking at creating your own job, and showing what you can do (ideally in real life so you get some more credibility). Be creative in approaching the right people, as that can get you noticed and can open doors. Show your talents off.

Use social media to get to know your potential clients much better. Follow them on twitter, Instagram or LinkedIn. But don't forget that these are social media — so you will need to engage, and give first before you take! Don't oversell yourself.

One of the hardest things about starting out is that you lack credibility and profile. What can you do so that the right people get to know you and trust you? Create a list of 10 companies you want to work for, research them in depth, and then identify actions to raise your credibility and profile, and how to approach them. Can you send something in the post? Can you attend networking events where they will speak and ask a question? Can you network with them online?

Patricia van den Akker, www.thedesigntrust.co.uk

4.32

4.32 — 4.35

Vidar Olufsen's unique "Top Secret" résumé was created at a time very few design agencies were hiring, and the design market was flooded. Vidar knew that most of the designers he would be competing against would be sending out more than standard, plain A4 résumés, so if he was to get noticed, he had to do something completely different.

Studio: Vidar Olufsen

Website: www.vimodesign.no

"Good work gets good work…

When you're starting out, one of the most daunting factors is getting work. A lot of design companies spend vast amounts on new business development, but the best way to get work is to do great work! If you've done a job and the client is pleased, they will tell their colleagues. Their competitors will also see the work and want to know who did it. It's also a good idea to mix commercial work with self-initiated or charity projects as they offer an opportunity to show your range of creativity and, if you shout about it, can also create a buzz about the studio."

John Gelder, Eleven Design Consultants, www.elevendesign.co.uk

Top tips: Setting goals — questions to ask yourself

- Do you have a list of design firms you want to work for?

- Do you have contacts within the companies you'd like to work for? (For more, see sections on networking, self–promotion, social media.)

- Have you devised a way to make yourself known to the potential employer? (See self–promotion, page 70.)

- Do the skills you have match the needs of the employer? (If not, what can you do about this? Internships? Short courses? See page 50.)

- Is there opportunity to progress and grow?

4.33

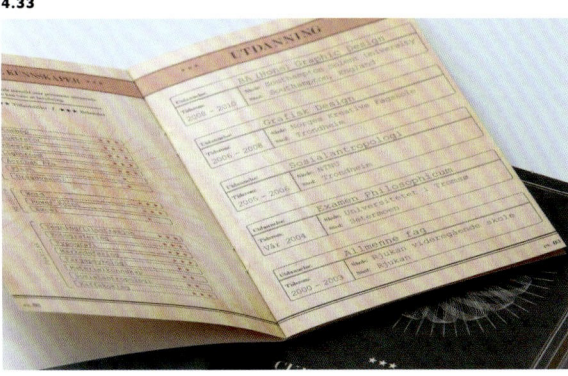

4.34

4.35

Your résumé

A résumé, together with a well-presented portfolio (see Chapter 3), is a precursor to obtaining a meeting that may lead to work and/or commissions. You need to make a good impression from the outset, so your résumé must be well designed, well-spaced and contain only precise and relevant information. Your résumé and covering letter are likely to be the first time that a potential client sees the way you handle typography, layout and color and they will make assumptions about your design ability based on these. As with any design job, always thoroughly check the copy to ensure there are no spelling or grammatical mistakes and that it has a good, logical structure. Many people believe that a résumé should be no more than two pages long so edit to fit. Attention to detail is an absolute must, especially when you are selling your skills.

Keep your résumé relevant and focus on your skills and previous experience that are most relevant to the job and use the terminology used in the job advert. Only include the most relevant work experience or skills and perhaps provide more detail about these rather than use up space adding in experience and skills that are not so relevant to the position you are applying for. Your résumé will grow and develop as your career grows and develops which means that you should periodically review and rewrite it to include your new skills, responsibilities and achievements.

It is often a good idea to start with a brief summary or profile paragraph that sums up your expertise and key skills and encapsulates your USP. Essential elements to include are contact details, skills, work experience and education, although it is fine to pick and choose the information you show. If you specialized in a certain area then you might want to list the courses or modules that hammer the point home as well as the jobs and duties that prove that you can fill the vacancy advertised. However, don't feel that you need to include every part-time position and summer job that you have ever had.

A résumé crime designers often commit is going over the top with design. Your portfolio is the place to showcase your design skills. In a résumé, interviewers want a clearly structured and functional document. Adding bells and whistles will be distracting and could mask important information. The task of a résumé is to get you through the door by showing that you have the right skills or profile that the employer is looking for. Nothing more and nothing less.

4.36 — 4.38
Business cards and fold-out résumé/portfolio.
Designer: Jamie Homer
Website: www.jamiehomer.co.uk

4.36

Top tips: What makes a good résumé?

- Target your résumé towards the job you are applying for, highlighting your skills, experience or enthusiasm that are required for the role.

- Ensure the layout is neat, organized and aesthetically pleasing. Check details, punctuation and spelling!

- Stick to one easy to read typeface and a couple of point sizes — only use type creatively if you are a graphic designer.

- Use substantial (not too flimsy) light colored or white paper.

- People will often meet your résumé before they meet you, so be sure to give a good impression!

www.artsthread.com

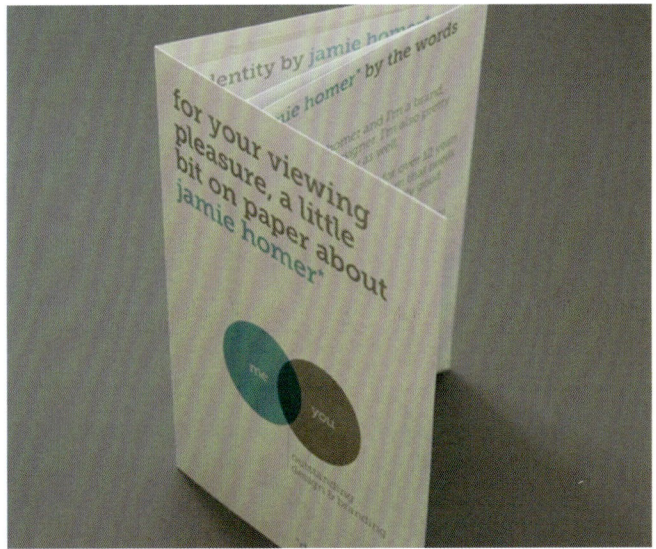

4.37

4.38

Interview skills

The interview stage is where a company shortlists the best of the applicants for final scrutiny. No matter how experienced you are, when you know an interview will decide whether or not you are going to get a job or commission, you will want it to go well. The key is preparation. Do your research. If an interviewer asks you about their company you need to be able to give an informed opinion and response about their business and market. If you have nothing to say they will assume you aren't very interested in working with them. With the information resources available on the Internet, there really is no excuse to not finding out about a potential employer and its business.

An interview is a conversation, not a test. You don't have to answer every question and know about each subject, but as long as you show a willingness to develop, listen and learn, you will do well. It's also the chance for you to ask questions and talk to the interviewer about what they do; the more interested you are in them, the more they will show interest in you. If your application is unsuccessful, make sure to ask for feedback, as this is key to your development as a designer and will likely signal weaknesses in skill areas that other employers are looking for. Try to act on this feedback, as showing willingness will put you in better stead for future positions at this company and others.

4.39

The "chat"

If a design studio calls you in for a chat, come armed with a portfolio and a knowledge of its past work and clients. No design studio has time to call people in just to say hi; if they have asked you to pop in it is because they are looking to expand their team, or need someone for a specific job. Do your research and find out what you can about them and the person you are meeting. Find out what department they are from, what their responsibilities are and which clients they work for. If possible, it is worth researching why and how the opportunity came about. For example, is it a new position or replacing someone who has left? It is okay to ask this at the interview, though you will receive a guarded response. Most positions come about because people have moved on to new opportunities, but if staff are leaving for other reasons, this could impact the desirability of the job. Researching the company will help you target your portfolio and prepare some talking points. Have an opinion about the company's work, and while you don't want to be too critical, you may prove your value by pointing out opportunities. Lastly, when you are asked to come in for a chat, this isn't a formal interview, so dress smart/casual — no suits!

"Learn to argue; self-belief is key. Be proud of your own work and be prepared to tell others why. I think confidence and interest in your own field are crucial — you need to love your work for others to love it too. Learning how to argue your ideas is absolutely crucial with client work too: if you want to get your visions through with a client, you need to be able to tell them why."

Lotta Nieminen

"1) You have no idea what people actually do, day to day, in their jobs. Before deciding that one career or another suits you, actually find out what people on that path do.

2) There is no such thing as "good". Nobody will pay you to do something "good" — because that's just you dressing up your opinion. They will pay you for effective, appropriate, relevant, useful…. Learn the difference early.

3) The famous companies are not necessarily the best to work for. Find companies where you will be fulfilled, not where you will be envied. Fulfilled and ignored is better than envied but miserable."

Kevin Hassall, Our Man in Belgrade

4.39
Portfolio review.
Facilitator: Arts Thread
Website: www.artsthread.com

5.1

5.1

This commission from Book Week Scotland, was to design a temporary facade for Inverness Library to help promote reading in Scotland. Each surface was decorated with layered shapes, colors, and textures to create new dimensions to the library's architecture. These illustrative "explorations of the imagination" were designed to convey the strong links between imagination and reading. The mural was successfully received by the community, who chose to keep this artwork installed, with the added benefit that it has solved their previous issues of graffiti, and community engagement.

Designer: Gabriella Marcella

Website: www.gabriellamarcella.com

Client: Inverness Library

5.2

Monthly promotional material for *NICE'N'SLEAZY*.

Designer: Gabriella Marcella

Website: www.gabriellamarcella.com

Client: NICE'N'SLEAZY

CHAPTER 5
THE WORKPLACE

Workplaces vary greatly depending on the type of design industry you work in. Office-style set-ups full of desks and desktops are still the way many large studios operate but they can be unaffordable for start-up companies and freelances, so shared or co-working spaces might be a better option. While design increasingly requires access to and the use of computer technology, powerful laptops and more affordable design software, coupled with the increased availability and power of Wi-Fi networks allow designers to be more mobile and to work virtually. This has greatly extended the definition of the studio and it can now encompass working from coffee shops, co-working spaces and home. While you can work in a coffee shop, most designers prefer to work in a space where they have reference materials, past work and creature comforts close at hand.

5.2

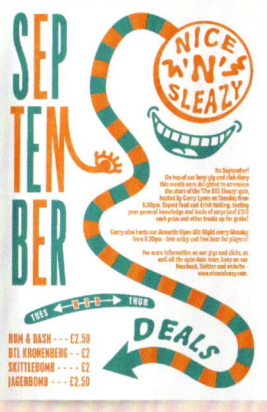
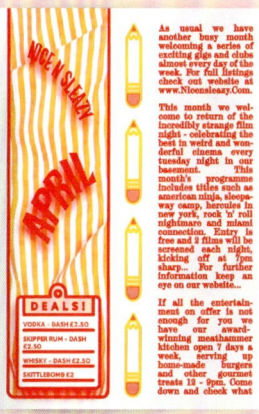

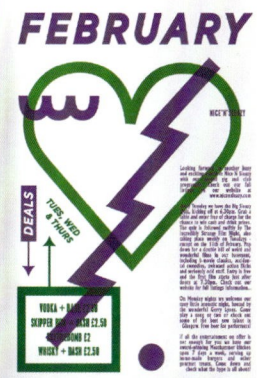

In this chapter we will:

- *Look at different workplace set-ups.*
- *Identify typical roles within the design industry, beyond just "designer".*

The traditional design agency

The title of this section is misleading, as there is no such thing as a traditional design agency. Previously, it was easy to define companies as marketing, advertising, branding and so on, and you could have gone to a design agency with almost any design project and they could have done it. Now it is almost impossible to apply such general terms (although there are some exceptions) as the industry has become increasingly specialized. If you want a print job, you go to a print design specialist; if you want a website you go to a web design specialist; if you want various things you go to a create concept designer and they will probably subcontract specific parts to other specialist firms that reflect the distinctions and specialization between print and digital. In a similar vein, when we talk about advertising it now covers anything from print ads in the local paper to integrated media campaigns, including the use of viral and ambient media.

Agencies may now seek to define and differentiate themselves by how they treat a brief and the thought processes they employ. Another difference may be the size and type of client they attract; a large agency might be categorized as "full service" whereas smaller competitors could brand themselves as "boutique" and make their size and specialization a unique selling point.

5.3
Shedio™ Studio.
Studio: Planning Unit
Website: www.planningunit.co.uk
5.4 + 5.5
Planning Unit's second studio space.
Studio: Planning Unit
Website: www.planningunit.co.uk

5.3

5.4

5.5

The design studio

A design studio is more than a physical space; it is a structured system with a dynamic flow that is conducive to the generation and realization of ideas. This structure and flow changes from studio to studio, and each has their own unique way of approaching client briefs and projects, and managing staff.

Studios will differ for many reasons, but chief among these is the nature of the work and the ethos of the company's founders. Traditionally a company that is predominately web-based would require a different physical set-up to a print-based studio. However, many contemporary design firms will cater for both print and web (and more); you will find bespoke sections in the same building with different equipment, set-ups and even varying management styles.

The ethos of the studio will set the tone and shape how the space is used. Some design firms will have a completely open and free-flowing approach to projects, whereas others will be more hierarchical and designate teams for certain tasks and take a more structured approach. This is always reflected in the make-up of the space. A company may feel it is best for colleagues to work without barriers between them to facilitate communication and sharing, so the space may be designed with few walls and more communal spaces and areas where ideas can be discussed.

When looking for work at a studio it is a good idea to have a look around the space and see how it is organized. Does it make you feel comfortable? This will give you the best indication of what it will be like to work there. For everyone this is a very personal choice, it should reflect how you approach design and whether the atmosphere will encourage your most creative work. For example, the design department of a well-known stock photo library in London is open plan with desks organized in work groups, facilitating communication between staff.

5.6

In the run up to Glasgow International 2014, Gabriella Marcella collaborated with MAP to create a new identity and design for their production of *A Feminist Chorus*. A pattern was created that could be broken down, blown up and used throughout the promotional material, events and publication. It brought unity to the wide range of sources included, and gave a distinct visual stamp on all their outputs. It was printed and designed in-house at Risotto Studio using the unique aesthetic associated with Risograph printers.

Designer: Gabriella Marcella

Website: www.gabriellamarcella.com

Client: MAP

5.7

Risotto Studio: Risograph print and design Specialist, Glasgow.

Designer: Gabriella Marcella

Website: www.gabriellamarcella.com

5.6

5.8

5.9

5.8 — 5.11

Uniform is a creative consultancy based in Liverpool, with additional offices in Clerkenwell, London.

Uniform's Liverpool stylish, monochrome base was designed by Snook Architects and makes use of reclaimed furniture and the odd splash of color within its open plan, multipurpose loft space.

Studio: Uniform

Website: www.uniform.net

Photograpy: Andy Haslam

5.10

5.11

SPOTLIGHT ON... ACMÉ PARIS

Tell us a bit about yourself.

We are two artistic directors, with common and complementary aspirations and universe of references. We met over two years ago, we quickly had the desire to work together. ACMÉ is the acronym of our two names, but it also means "a company who makes everything", and it well suits us because it opens things to endless possibilities!

When you get a new brief in, is there a particular process you follow?

At the beginning we share artistic references with our client (it can be graphic design but also photography, fashion, architecture, movies...) and also the aesthetic universes they're receptive/sensitive to. Then we want to know which values they want to pass on. We use it as a compass throughout the project.

At this point, we do research on the subject (as widely as possible) and start to play with graphic shapes, but separately. When we feel that we are going around in circles we exchange files and slowly, like pouring material through a sieve, we end up by refining forms and ideas. At this point, we feel that we are ready to show our work to the client!

Your work has a very strong coherent feel even though it spans a range of specialisms; was this a conscious decision, or did the work lead you?

It's not really deliberate from us, it's more what others see that made us realize this unity (which is kind of pleasant). It's like building your own personality, you don't really decide who you are or who you want to be, but at the end everybody is coherent within themselves, right? The thing is that we love working with typography, playing with letters and we really paid attention to all of the visual production line: paper and printing techniques, it can convey as much meaning as graphic shapes.

You have some wonderful, high profile clients. How did you go about developing this base?

It's several chance meetings, word-of-mouth and wonderful encounters. We are really bad at canvassing, so we have to let destiny do it this way and it's quite pleasant! People call us because they know our work and they appreciate it, so they're more receptive to our ideas!

ACMÉ has retained a small studio identity and you remain involved in projects right the way through the process. Is keeping that overview important to the way you work?

Of course ! It's part of our pleasure and why ACMÉ was created. So we can follow conscientiously each project from a client calling with a new request to the delivery of the printed objects (or online if it's a website!).

We love to work closely with providers (printers, paper suppliers, developers...), dialog is always rewarding and helps to push further projects and ideas. (And we are control freaks so we like to have an eye on each step to be sure of a perfect result.)

The skills required by the various projects you work on must be vast. Do you find much commonality, or is each way of working very distinct?

We kind of always work the same way, the important thing is to be aware of the client's needs, answer his requests, doubts and questions, and always keep in mind his first request to be sure to stay the course. (Sometimes there is turbulence, but it always ends up in the right place!)

How do you find time to keep developing new skills?

We're both really curious and not just in graphic design... One of the reason we love our job, is that we can work for fashion, literature, gastronomy, or any kind of area and learn new things every day!

5.12

For skills relating to our area of activity, we always find time because we quickly get a feeling of going around in circles if we rest on our laurels. This is done naturally!

You take a playful approach to your work, how do you maintain this sensibility and keep up with client demands?

For us playing is an integral part of creativity. We can be a bit discouraged sometimes (fortunately it rarely happens). In this situation we talk of chucking everything and opening an underground bar where you can also buy plants and design furniture. Thinking of it always brings our working back on track!

5.12 — 5.14

Hands is a new animation studio, where the manual aspect (as you can guess), proximity and the willingness to serve the client in the fairest way are absolutely essential.

We thus made a logo with each letter embodying a figure with its own mood. We then decided to use colorful papers to bring the nice and human aspect of the studio forwards, and artisanal silkscreen printing to further emphasize the project's nature.

Studio: ACMÉ Paris

Website: www.acme-paris.com

Client: HANDS

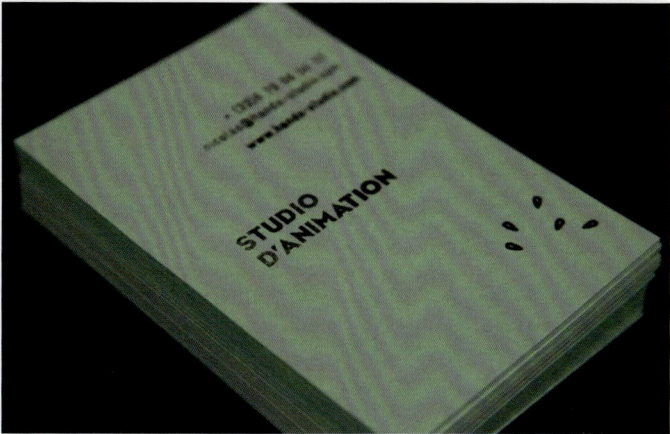

5.13

5.14

Studio roles

A design studio is an organism of many parts that does not function well if some strands are missing. Let's start at the top. Each agency will have some form of management — without management, nothing will get done. Depending upon its business needs, this may just be the founding partners in a boutique studio or it could be a range of executives responsible for creative, technology, business development, finance and so on, in larger firms. Although not necessarily true for smaller or boutique design studios, once most organizations reach a certain size, they naturally have to become hierarchical as the owner or partner is unable to manage everything themselves. In larger organizations, each section or team will have a leader or manager who is responsible for assigning work, ensuring that work gets done on time, attending planning meetings and dealing with studio business. In smaller organizations, however, management functions may fall to the more senior staff, yet many designers just want to get on with the task at hand and be creative and do not want to be burdened with this.

Designers may have many different titles, but the three most common are junior, middleweight and senior designer.

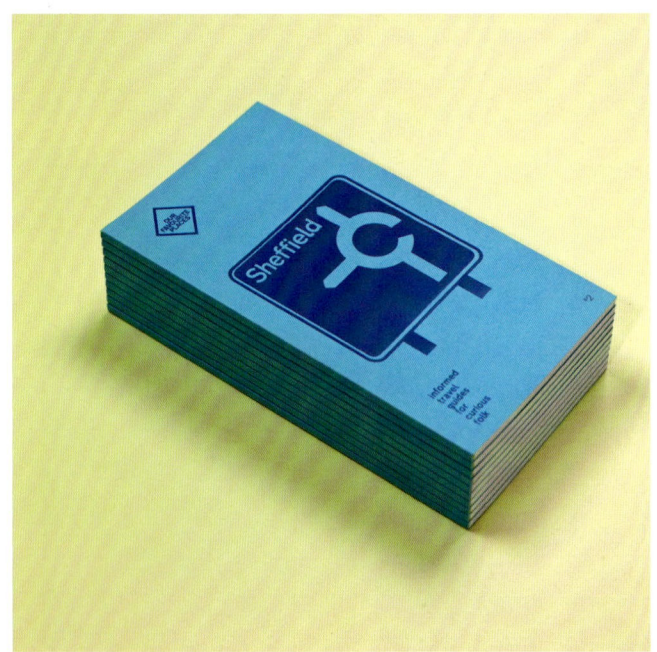

5.15

5.16

Junior designer

A junior designer will be a recent graduate, or someone new to the industry. Normally they will be responsible for artworking and executing the ideas of more senior designers. The juniors will be mentored by, and work closely with, senior and middleweight designers. Skills are very important when you are looking for a job at this level. You will need to be able to artwork ideas swiftly and for this you will need to have a good knowledge of the right software and technical processes required. The broader your skill set, the more likely you are to land a junior designer role.

Middleweight designer

A middleweight designer will be a few years into their career and on the way up. The title indicates that they are a designer with experience and ability. They may have started out as a junior designer within the company and been promoted or joined from another company at this level. A good artworker is the equivalent of a middleweight designer. Though an artworker may not generate concepts, they do address important technical issues and ensure that work is sent on correctly. They will get work ready for print and have a very good knowledge of pre-press requirements such as file types and color balances. This is a very important and often overlooked role, but a good artworker can save a company a lot of money by making sure things don't have to be reprinted.

Senior designer

A senior designer will head up creative projects and decide on the direction of a project together with the creative and art directors. As the title suggests, they are senior in the company and therefore experienced. This status is not always dependent on age as a talented designer may be promoted swiftly to this level because of their evident creative and conceptual skills. A senior designer will work with the account manager and studio manager to ensure that good ideas are presented to clients. Teams made up of senior, middleweight and junior designers will then execute these ideas. The senior designer will take ownership of the project and be responsible for its progress and the quality of the work.

5.15 + 5.16

Eleven Design's *Our Favourite Places* (OFP) is a guidebook that celebrates their home city. *OFP* is a self-initiated project by their studio and all design, illustration and writing is done by their team.

Eleven Design created *OFP* to encourage people to visit their lovely, hilly home city. As well as these books they made a short film, devised a series of walking tours, created a Sheffield alphabet, published a Sheffield coloring book and created an online city guide.

For more: www.ourfaveplaces.bigcartel.com

Studio: Eleven Design

Website: www.elevendesign.co.uk

These are general job titles or ranks, but the work they do can be very different in different studios. In smaller companies a senior designer will often take on some account management duties, while in a larger organization they will just design. In the same way, expectations of junior designers vary greatly. Some will be expected to artwork only, whereas others will be more involved in creative decisions.

How do you know which role will suit you best? As a new entrant to the industry, you will probably start in a junior role and work your way up as you develop experience. This will give you time to see which aspects of the job you like best. Maybe you will find that you like managing design projects more than actual designing, or vice versa. However, you should regularly examine your skills set and best assets to see how you would like your career to progress and what you need to improve in order to move in the direction you want to.

Account manager

An account manager is tasked with bringing work in. They stay in close contact with clients and liaise between design teams to make sure that the work gets done. To be successful in this role a person needs to be approachable and a good communicator as well as highly organized. An account manager has the closest relationship with the client of all the workers in the studio. From doing the initial pitching of ideas through to final delivery, the account manager will be the client's main point of contact. Before the work goes out the door, it is also the account manager's responsibility to check it thoroughly to ensure that it meets the brief, so attention to detail is a vital skill to have.

It may sound strange, but a designer may actually have very little contact with the client. This allows them to focus on the work and provides a buffer in that client feedback can be relayed to the designer by the account manager without the emotion a client might bring to a meeting or the time-impact that a meeting would have. Feedback, channelled via the account manager, can thus be delivered in a way that the designer can interpret and work with.

The number of clients an accounts manager will look after depends largely on the size of the agency. In smaller agencies a single person might look after all of the clients, but in a larger agency with bigger clients there will be several account managers, each with a portfolio of clients.

Studio manager

Most large agencies will have a studio manager to look after the day-to-day running of the studio, its requirements and even ordering new materials and resources. Normally the studio manager will interact with the various teams and ensure that everything is running effectively. Like account managers, they need to be highly organized and show great attention to detail. Even in small agencies, it is important that someone has this role to provide a constant overview of things, or deadlines can be missed.

Traffic manager

The role of the job of traffic manager overlaps with that of the studio manager, but their remit is normally more driven by communication with clients rather than with the designers. Their role is process driven as they chase designers for the work and hurry them along when deadlines are pressing. Once the account manager has brought in the work, the traffic manager books in the job, allocates times and then monitors progress.

5.17

The first floor of Clearleft's beautifully lit office and auditorium.

Studio: Clearleft Ltd

Website: www.clearleft.com

5.18

A-Design Lab's studio space.

"Visual loveliness it is important — we like to be surrounded by inspiring things like motivational frames, Rubik cube and our adorable Munny (a white vinyl toy) that has become the mascot of the studio. Oh, and we love plants."

Studio: A-Design Lab Ltd

Website: www.a-designlab.com

5.17

5.18

Creative director

The key responsibility for a creative director is heading the design strategy for the agency. Many creative companies will have a creative director whose primary responsibility is to oversee and filter design and client decisions. This may include selecting which clients to take on and the type of work done for them, i.e. is the company going to concentrate on web or print services, or provide a full design service? They will give the company its emphasis and often decide its look and feel. Their role is almost that of company guru as they are often brought in because they are associated with a certain style or type of work and are expected to bring this knowledge to the role. In boutique firms, one of the founders or one of the partners is also typically the creative director. Creative director is the natural progression from senior designer or art director. To take on this role you'll need to be a good leader and manager in addition to having an attractive creative vision.

Art director

An art director heads up the creative teams, implements the vision, develops concepts and ultimately makes sure that the work meets the requirements of the client. They work across creative departments and disciplines, so it can be a very wide-ranging position. Management skills are key to this role, but additionally you will need the ability to influence and inspire others and encourage them to make the best work possible. It is an art director's job to encourage and mentor designers, so it is important that they enjoy working with people.

Design director

A design director will work within the purview of the creative director. They often will work under their guidance and make on-the-ground choices about which jobs are chosen and which are refused. Essentially, they find the way of executing the vision of the creative director and work between them and the art director.

5.19 — 5.22

Planning Unit were asked to create a consistent visual language — a suite of icons — to be introduced to the BBC's most popular areas: iPlayer, Sport, News, Travel, Children's, Weather and Social. The suite would be used in every aspect of the BBC's digital space and formed the vocabulary of its Global Experience Language.

The final result presents a suite of 180 icons; a modern and cohesive showcase of what the BBC currently represents in its digital evolution.

Studio: Planning Unit

Website: www.planningunit.co.uk

Client: BBC

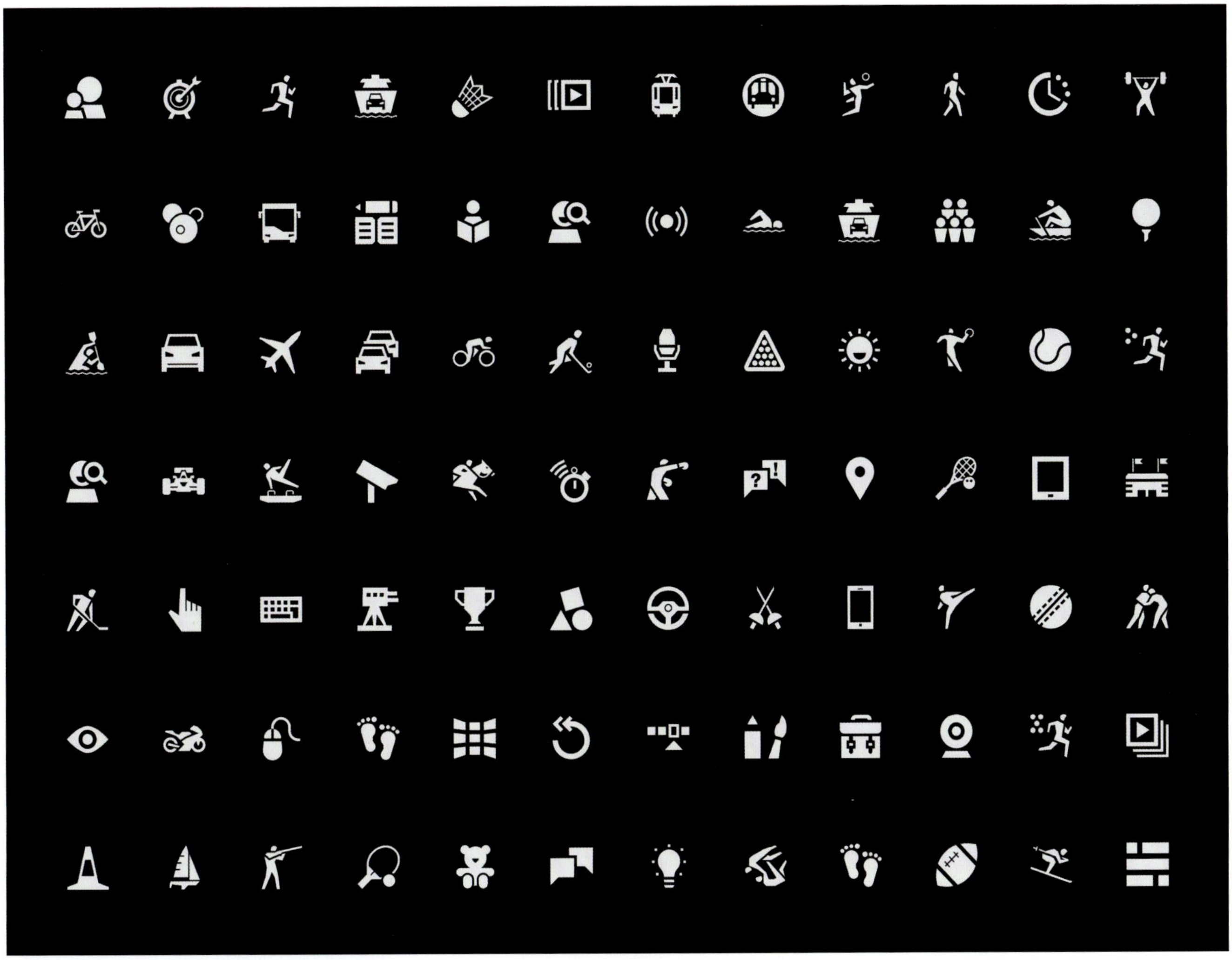

5.19

5.20

5.21

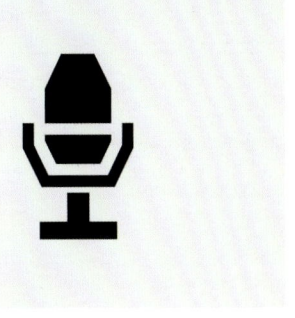

5.22

Web designers and developers

The web is an area that has developed so quickly and become so important that most design studios will have an individual or team that works solely on this. In addition to basic HTML and CSS skills, a designer in this area will need a good knowledge of associated technologies such as PHP, MySQL, Java and content management systems, and keep abreast of all relevant developments. Agencies may also have multimedia designers who will look at apps, interactive displays and other emerging technologies. Even the design of interfaces for websites and apps can be so specialist that user-experience experts are needed.

A front-end designer will look after the design of websites using Photoshop, or basic HTML and CSS. They are responsible for generating the visual look of a website and determining what its functional elements are. While the front-end developer might suggest interactive qualities, it is unlikely they will contribute towards the development of this functionality. Additionally, the designer will have to consider how the designs look and function on a variety of devices, from mobile phones to super desktops.

The back-end designer then takes this design and makes it work. They will work with the elements created by the front-end designer and generate the code needed to make the pages function, including the addition of functionality such as interactivity, databases, animation and more.

Interactivity is present in many more locations than websites, such as kiosks, mobile phones and tablets. This growth has led to the development of many specialist roles, and key amongst these are UX (User Experience) specialists who will look after the user journey and UI (User Interface) designers who look after graphic elements such as buttons, forms and navigation. UX will be measured through rigorous testing managed by the UX specialist.

5.23

Other design roles

Roles in any given agency may overlap, but there are some areas that require such specialized skills that freelancers with specialist knowledge are hired to come in and help the company.

Exhibition design, for example, involves specialist insight and knowledge, even architectural skills and knowledge of construction methods and materials because it requires building physical installations.

A niche role that is constantly in demand is for packaging designers. This also requires very specific knowledge of materials and construction methods, albeit on a smaller scale, but as packaging has grown to emphasize the brand experience (Apple's enticing packaging is a great example of this) areas of interactivity and branding are often incorporated.

The term 'typographer' may refer to a person who works with type or someone who designs typefaces. The design of type is a very specialized skill and requires a different skill set and a much higher attention to detail than that held by many graphic designers. A typeface designer may create work for a specific client or commission, but many will design fonts without a specific brief that a graphic designer will find a use for in a future design task.

Copywriters help shape the message and create the text used in designs, assisting clients in phrasing their messages and writing advertising copy and blog entries, webpages, social media updates and more.

Illustrators often work alongside designers helping to demonstrate and render concepts, or creating unique artwork for projects. 3D designers do this in three dimensions, for example, to show what an exhibition space or new store or building development will look like.

Beyond this, projects will regularly call for experts in marketing, public relations, advertising and branding, especially when it comes to larger briefs with substantial, high-profile clients.

5.23

Website redesign for *Lula*, a UK-based fashion magazine.

Art Direction & Design: Lotta Nieminen

Website: www.lottanieminen.com

Client: Lula

5.24 + 5.25

Some "snapshots" of Suisse studio.

The studio is on the top floor of a building in Glasgow's Merchant City. It's a beautiful space, clients often comment on how wonderful it feels when they come in for meetings. It's a relaxing space, a happy, creative place.

Studio: Suisse

Website: www.suissestudio.com

5.24

5.25

Human resources

Human resources will play a part in any business once it grows to a size that it can support its cost. A good HR department will alleviate many daily management stresses that get in the way of projects and take managers away from the creative business. This team will look after employee and third-party contracts and processes essential to the survival of the company. While they may not find new talent, they will ensure the new member of staff is paid, trained and that they are eligible to do the work (in terms of national law), and help resolve workplace disputes.

New talent

As the company grows, bringing in new talent is essential. When looking for new creative employees a company can go to degree shows, advertise, hire a recruitment consultant, or seek recommendations from existing employees. To assist in this search, the new talent team will be scouring blogs and social media, forging links with universities and looking at ways to poach talent from rival firms.

Marketing and business development

Another responsibility that becomes more important once an agency grows is marketing and new business development. While account managers might be out talking to potential clients, marketing and business development teams look for ways to grow the company by identifying new markets to compete in. On a day-to-day basis they may run social media accounts, work with external companies to find outlets for promotional messaging and seek other opportunities to push the studio brand forward.

5.26

5.27

5.26 — 5.28

In the summer of 2014, Sweden's #1 microbrewery PangPang wanted to develop a summer beer series. Snask built a marketing and packaging concept around the idea of tiki and named the beers Cocojambo, Pelekane, Bamboleo, Libertango, Playa del Drevviken, Waikiki, Flamingo-GO, and Tiki Tango. The use of smart branding, eye-catching colors and gorgeous design helped PangPang beat its competitors and raise their profile.

Studio: Snask

Website: www.snask.com

Client: PangPang Brewery

Support roles

There are many support roles and services that a design studio depends upon and maintaining good relationships with them is essential if you expect them to help you out when things go wrong or you face a particularly challenging job. Printers continue to play a key role in production. As soon as a project requires duplication of an artifact (a brochure or poster, for example), it is generally not cost-effective for a studio to invest in the relevant specialist equipment, so they send it to an expert. Most printing companies have a representative who works with design firms to ensure that they get the quality of printed product they require. Once a good relationship is established, this collaboration can be mutually beneficial for both parties; the printer will get repeat business and the design firm will have a person they trust on speed dial.

Web-hosting companies have become a resource as sought after as good printers. Hosting a website (or multiple sites) takes a lot of power and technological expertise, as well as a dedicated team running things. But once a relationship has been established, many design firms may end up renting a large amount of website space capacity from the host that they will then divide among their clients and charge back for at a premium.

Many design agencies also employ freelancers to fill skills gaps or temporarily increase their design team when it is necessary. Skills that are commonly sought after include web developers, illustrators, photographers and copywriters. Working as a freelancer in any one of these industries can be extremely lucrative and lead to a varied and exciting career.

5.28

SPOTLIGHT ON… JOSHUA OGDEN, AKQA

Tell us a bit about yourself.

I am currently a creative at AKQA based in London. My work is equally balanced between concepting, copywriting and designing. I am massively inspired by architecture.

Could you detail the steps that led to your current career?

At university I got space and time to experiment. I wasn't afraid of failing or producing work that didn't lead to anything. It's that "dare to fail" mentality that lead onto the project I worked on for D&AD which went onto win.

Winning the 2013 D&AD Student of the year opened the door for me. The opportunities after doing a project that gained such recognition came quickly, it was overwhelming. Job offers and interviews came quick and fast. The hard part was deciding what and where to go.

I was contacted quickly by the judge from D&AD, Ian Wharton, who was interested in finding out what I was up to and what my next steps were. As a result, he put me in contact with founder and CEO of AKQA, Ajaz Ahmed. One of AKQA's key foundations is about having the best talent, and he saw in me a diverse set of skills needed for such a fast paced industry and he welcomed me to join AKQA as a creative. Ian joined the same day as Creative Director and we started a small team within the agency.

What's the single best thing about your job?

I don't really have a typical day. The project dictates the type of work and even the location. I usually have between three and four projects running. These vary between pitches and client work.

I love that my role is so broad. My work ranges from digital design/editorial design/interaction/art directing film and even interior design concepts. Also, I have a beautiful workspace.

What tips would you offer to students looking to break into the industry?

I believe I wouldn't have my position without a broad portfolio. Agencies know students straight out of education are not going to know everything, and they possibly already have 50 other people with great web design and development skills. So you need to show creativity and the ability to adapt. Agencies really value a fresh approach.

Keep experimenting. If you can maintain the same enthusiasm and excitement that you had in education you will produce ground-breaking work in industry.

Tell us about *Justified* magazine:

Some friends and I had a blog at university; it was about promoting up-and-coming work. Issue one took off and lead to issue two.

Then we all started work… (Jasper and Will included).

Things slowed. We just didn't feel that inspired to continue with it. We were all so focused on client work that the mag took a back seat.

It wasn't until about nine months ago that I realized that a massive part of what I do for AKQA, and the role of being a good art director, is about finding and keeping on top of not only cultural references but artists and photographers that have that unique angle, which was also the core of *Justified*. The new refined mission statement is — "*Justified* magazine searches for only the most original and compelling work. The result is a showcase of beautiful photography, set design, styling and image-making".

I love that fact that now *Justified* is like my own personal physical blog of inspiration. Every creative has been selected so meticulously that if someone were to say who/what inspires you I could just hand them the latest copy of *Justified*. What is also great is that I am starting to use/propose the creatives in the magazine for projects at AKQA. It works.

So, that's where *Justified* is at present. We are pretty excited and motivated to keep it alive. It's super important for us to have it. Will and Jasper are now pretty big print designers in branding and editorial (Jasper works for *The Telegraph*) so for them to have this canvas to play is cool to see.

5.31

5.32

5.29

5.30

5.29 + 5.30

Images of Joshua's workspace at AKQA.

Studio: AKQA

Website: www.akqa.com

5.31 + 5.32

Justified, a showcase of beautiful photography, set design, styling and image-making. Forever in print.

Designer: Joshua Ogden

Website: www.joshuaogden.com/

6.1

6.2

6.1 — 6.3

Personal branding for freelance graphic designer, Claire Bruining. Detailing the creative process that led to this work, Claire said:

"I have always loved the idea of simplicity and order amongst chaos and I really wanted my identity to be strong and refined yet playful. Initially I had no vision for the end result, so I just started by experimenting with color, composition and shape, embracing chance and chaos."

Designer: Claire Bruining

Website: www.behance.net/clairebruining

CHAPTER 6
GOING FREELANCE

The freedom to shape your own future is the key attraction for many designers when they think about working for themselves, whether as a freelance or starting their own design agency. These forms of working share a lot of similarities but also some notable differences as you will see throughout this chapter. For many creatives, working freelance effectively means working as a one–person agency, the only difference being scale (one person can only do so much). This chapter aims to set out some of the main considerations to take into account when contemplating working for yourself.

6.3

In this chapter we will:

- Assess the pros and cons of freelance life.
- Talk about different work set–ups as a freelancer.
- Consider ways in which to take your first steps to becoming a business owner.

Working freelance

If you are motivated, confident and looking for variety, a freelance career might be the best option for you. Freelancers can work directly with clients or in–house for an agency. Both can be lucrative, but be aware that to be successful requires a great deal of dedication, hard work and organization.

Managing your own career can be a great way to start out as a designer as you will make all the client, design and financial decisions. By working as a freelancer directly with your own clients, you'll experience all of the roles such as design, account management, project management and more that are undertaken in a studio, and additionally you will have to take on administration, marketing and promotion responsibilities.

Starting out as a freelancer can be quite daunting for a recent graduate as you will be competing against larger design companies and seasoned freelancers with established track records and years of experience. But you will have advantages. Being a freelancer means you will be cheaper than a design agency and if you have recently graduated your knowledge may be more current than that of some practicing designers. Lack of real–world experience can also be a positive as your ideas may be freer and more diverse than those of an experienced designer who plays it safe and sticks to a tried and tested approach.

Getting work will depend on the strength of your portfolio and your ability to self–promote and network (see Chapter 3). Even if you don't have lots of real–world projects to show, competition briefs, live briefs undertaken at university and even jobs for family and friends will show your ability to work to a brief and create quality outcomes. You probably won't find work with large corporations straight out of university, but smaller companies and freelancers in other creative disciplines, such as photography and illustration, will need your skills and will be looking to work with people like you.

Working freelance can be quite isolating as you will spend a great deal of your time working alone from home. There are ways to mitigate this however, such as working with another freelancer or joining a collective with other designers to create a studio environment. Being part of a collective also means that you can pitch for work together and take on larger commissions that require a wider skills set than you can provide alone. Sharing a working space can also be rewarding as you get the social interaction as well as the ability to share ideas, and possibly even work leads.

As a freelancer, the buck stops with you for any work that you do and you will have to resolve any problems without the support from co–workers. As a one–person business, your ability to grow is limited by your ability to work quickly and efficiently. Taking a break or a vacation may also mean having to turn down or miss out on work and the possibility that your clients will find someone else to work with in your absence. Lack of physical capacity is one reason why some freelancers decide to form a design studio and bring more people on board.

Top tips: Freelance career checklist

- Register as being self–employed
- Set up a bookkeeping system
- Consider your rates
- Find a place to work

- Grow your network
- Develop your website and branding
- Get out and meet clients
- Make great work

Managing a freelance career

The freelance life will see you face many of the same challenges as designers who start their own studios, albeit on a smaller scale. You will be responsible for your own administration such as billing clients and chasing payments. You will always have an element of financial uncertainty due to the irregularity of work coming in, which will be multiplied if you are tardy billing clients or shy about chasing payment. When you start out, depending on your circumstances, it may be necessary to have other sources of income available to get you through quiet periods or until you have built up a financial cushion.

Managing your freelance career isn't just about taking care of your money; you will also have to look after every aspect of your business from getting work to chasing invoices. To be able to do this you should have a plan and clear objectives (both short– and long–term).

Creating a business plan will help you to be clear about your objectives and goals, and identifying the smaller steps that you need to take in order to achieve these. Ask yourself what kind of work do you want to create and for which type of client or sector do you want to undertake this work? Even

if you hope to keep your area of expertise broad, it is useful to decide on a specific type of client with whom you would like to work. Having an area of specialism is ideal as there is nothing worse than introducing yourself as someone who does a bit of everything for anyone who asks. This doesn't instill confidence in a potential client. There is more information about business planning later in this chapter in the section about starting your own design studio.

Freelance pros	
Be your own boss	Choose your working hours
Work from anywhere	Choose your clients
Escape office politics	Choose your working hours

Freelance cons	
The buck stops with you	Growth is linked to your capacity for work
Gaining sizeable clients can be difficult	Taking a break means turning down work
Lone working can be solitary	Tax returns...

Deciding whether to go freelance is a life-changing decision. For all of the freedom it affords you, there is much to do aside from making creative work. The above table may help you decide if it's the right choice for you.

Being your own account manager

One of the most challenging aspects of the freelance life is taking on the roles associated with running a graphic design business and finding the time to do them as well as designing. Managing clients, getting in new business and undertaking administrative responsibilities is time-consuming, but essential. You will need to develop your own systems to handle this (a diary, white board, calendar and other systems — be creative!), but as your freelance business grows some of this can be outsourced.

One thing many freelancers don't consider early on is keeping track of projects. When you work in a studio, the studio manager or traffic manager will keep track of work, deadlines and progress, but when you work alone it is easy to get excited about one project and forget you have other jobs on. There are many workflow applications that can help with this, but equally a white board and Post–it notes can be effective tracking tools.

Communicating with clients can also take up considerable time, so be disciplined and find a way to do this effectively to save yourself time. Requests and information can often get lost in email chains and avoiding this is the first step to keeping on top of projects. Managing the way clients give you feedback can save you from having to deal with flurries of short, bitty emails. You could request a weekly conversation, or look at task–based web software that can be easily accessed by both parties and managed as a central resource.

6.4 + 6.5

The Guild offers a mixture of creative and meeting rooms. Housed in the Grade I listed former Tech College at the Guildhall, the Guild is a new co–working space (hot–desking) designed for the those working in either the tech or creative industries.

Venue: Co–working Bath — The Guild

Website: www.theguildhub.co.uk

"You don't need to go to a large city to be successful.

Because of the improvements in communication (Skype/video calling, etc.) and services such as Dropbox, Github, etc. people can work remotely with much more ease than they could in the past. There are also so many design/digital hubs around the country now as it has become much more widespread in the last 10 years or so, so you don't need to gravitate towards the capital to find that. Sure, you may not have the paycheck of someone who works in London or New York, but you also won't have the extortionate prices or the crushing commute to your place of work."

Michelle Dinan, designer and front–end dev, michelledinan.com

Co–working and Collectives

If you want to work for yourself, but find it hard to remain motivated working from home, finding a co–working space can be a good solution. Co–working relates to groups of (often creative) people who work for themselves in a rented space alongside others who are similarly self–employed. It can also be an alternative way to surround yourself with experts.

A co–working space is more than just rows of desks as a good co–working space will offer opportunities for collaborative projects and career development. When using the work space you sit alongside other creative people in a creative environment and this will often spur you on, much as working in the computer lab or design studio at university did. Such spaces also provide a forum to discuss ideas and concepts, ask for help and tips, and learn new technical or creative skills. Many co–working spaces also put on seminars to help their members with more complex business issues and to develop their careers. Inspirational talks may be offered or activities such as Pecha Kuchas (concise, fast–paced presentations pioneered in Tokyo) or show–and–tell sessions so that people can come together as a community, share ideas and talk about projects.

There are many other types of events that will help you develop a supportive network and grow your skills. Hack events can be a lot of fun in terms of blue sky thinking and open ended creativity.

A collective is a group of freelancers who pool together so that they can take on larger clients, and splinter off when they get smaller projects. This can be a really useful way to work as it simulates the design studio feel, but offers the individuality and freedom of a freelance career. Collectives can also be more disparate in the range of members — in one group you might find illustrators, filmmakers and fine artists.

6.4

6.5

SPOTLIGHT ON... JESSICA HISCHE

Tell us a bit about yourself.

I'm a letterer, illustrator, and type designer living in San Francisco (and occasionally also in Brooklyn). I began my career as a graphic designer (working under Louise Fili) but when I went off on my own I decided to focus on custom lettering work rather than continuing down a more traditional graphic design path. I've been working for myself since 2009 and have been able to work with amazing clients like Wes Anderson, Penguin Books, *The New York Times*, etc. and have been lucky enough to travel the world speaking about what I do at various conferences and colleges.

How does your career compare to the one you dreamt about as a student?

When I was in school, one of our assignments was to create our "dream résumé" from five years in the future. Mine involved working at a few design shops in Philly before moving on to work at Pentagram. Had I pursued that path (working at a larger design agency), I think my career would have turned out quite differently. All of the studios I've worked for have been tiny, and because of that I've had more direct mentorship than maybe I would have at a larger firm. Also, because I ended up working for Louise, who runs a tight ship and keeps very regular hours, I was able to pursue freelance work, which enabled me to go out on my own earlier than I likely would have had I worked at a bigger firm with more demanding hours.

In terms of your career path, how and when did you know you'd made a good decision?

I think as soon as I ended up at Tyler School of Art I felt like everything was going to be OK. I was encouraged by all of my teachers tremendously and hard work seemed to translate to opportunities (I was recommended for internships because of my work ethic, professors were always happy to offer advice/put in extra time to help me because they saw I tried so hard). I've had a few

bumps along my career path, but for the most part they were temporary hiccups not complete derailments. I generally judge my success by how happy I am on a daily basis, and so far that metric has been pretty good!

A lot of people will know you through the Daily Drop Cap. You must have a lot of great ideas, so how did you know this was one that you wanted to concentrate on (or put your efforts into), and did you have any idea how successful it would become?

With Daily Drop Cap, I just wanted to create a way for me to draw letters every day. I gave myself parameters (one letter a day (until 12 alphabets were complete), drawn in the morning, spending no more than two hours on it). It was easy to concentrate efforts on it and stick with it because I was getting outside encouragement. It would have been really hard to keep going after a few alphabets had I not felt accountable to people that were following the project. Whenever I make something, I need to have a "client" or at least an audience for that thing. I think that's what makes me love design so much and what pushed me away from fine art. I don't make work for myself, I make it for others. I just love bringing a little joy into people's days if I can through things I make. Most of my side projects have a specific audience in mind when I make them, for my wedding invitation it was my friends and family, for inkerlinker it was other designers looking for printers, for Don't Fear the Internet it was other people like me that wanted to learn how to build things on the web but were intimidated by the resources that existed.

How and when do you find time to develop yourself and keep learning?

I really have to push myself to keep developing. Because I do so much public speaking, I'm able to attend a lot of conferences and listening to other speakers usually puts a major fire under my butt to do better work. Sharing a studio with another hard—working (and super talented) letterer really pushes me to make new and interesting work. I find that I need to surround myself with people I look up to in one way or another. I never want to be the most interesting, talented, or hard–working person in the room.

What drives you to keep creating new work, seeking out collaborations and exploring fresh areas of design (for example, Don't Fear the Internet and the titles for *Moonrise Kingdom*)?

Moonrise Kingdom fell into my lap and because it was for Wes Anderson, a person whose work I deeply admire, I pushed myself to new levels, trusting that my type design skills were good enough to make something great under his tight art direction. I tend to explore other areas of design (like web design) when I have a specific project in mind. I learned web design to be able to build my own portfolio site and to launch personal projects without the help of a developer. I want to take poetry classes (I'm over thinking that poetry is cheesy), because I think that it will influence my lettering work.

Life is short and I've wound up in a unique position in the world (in that I'm able to make a living doing what I love and have a relatively flexible schedule as a freelancer), so I want to learn and do as much as I can while I'm here.

You are very good at self–promotion and letting people know about your exciting projects, is this a skill you've always had, or something you've developed out of necessity?

I think I've always been a relatively good communicator, but I definitely hope that when people see me talk about a project online they don't only think of it as "self–promotion". I just love to share my life with others and I love it when people share their lives with me. I'm genuinely interested in even the mundane daily activities of my friends and family, Russ (my husband) is always astounded when I ask him detailed questions about his day.

6.6

After working with Dave Eggers on *A Hologram for the King* I was pumped to be brought on board to design his new book, *The Circle*. It was especially fun to design this cover, as I've spent the last two years living in San Francisco surrounded by the tech industry (my husband works for Facebook) and the story is set in an influential social media company. I also had to design a logo for the fictitious company, The Circle, and was inspired by the interweaving connectivity of social media sites and also knots that once tight are difficult to untie.

Designer: Jessica Hische

Website: www.jessicahische.is

Clients: McSweeney's/Knopf

6.6

SPOTLIGHT ON... JESSICA HISCHE

Who, or what is your biggest inspiration?

One of the things that inspires me most to keep going and build up a career for myself is that I love being independent. My mom gave up her career to raise my brother and I and has struggled through much of her adulthood to stay afloat financially. I want to be able to not only be financially independent but to be able to help my friends and family when they occasionally need a leg up.

What is the single best thing about your job?

I love that, just by doing what I love and sharing myself and my work with the world, I've been able to help younger designers on their path to pursuing their dreams. The emails that I occasionally get from struggling young designers motivate me to keep pushing myself, to keep writing articles, and to keep speaking/mentoring/teaching more than anything.

6.7 — 6.10

Penguin Drop Caps is a series of twenty—six collectible hardcover editions of fine works of literature, each featuring on its cover a specially commissioned illustrated letter of the alphabet by yours truly! A collaboration between myself and Penguin Art Director Paul Buckley, whose series design encompasses a rainbow—hued spectrum across all twenty—six books, Penguin Drop Caps debuted with an 'A' for Jane Austen's *Pride and Prejudice*, a 'B' for Charlotte Brontë's *Jane Eyre*, and a 'C' for Willa Cather's *My Ántonia*, and continues with more perennial classics from Penguin.

Designer: Jessica Hische

Website: www.jessicahische.is

Client: Penguin Books

6.7

6.8

6.9

6.10

6.11

6.11

I had the absolute honor of creating the film titles for Wes Anderson's film, *Moonrise Kingdom*. I worked directly with Wes and his small team of co–producers to bring his vision to life. The film is based in New England in the early 1960s. The initial direction was based on Ed Benguiat's Edwardian Script, but the direction shifted toward something more hand–hewn looking and lightly referencing titles from a Chabrol film. I was hired to create the 20 or so credits in the beginning of the movie, and a typeface to be used for the end credits. I ended up creating two fonts — a display and a text weight of the same typeface. Working with Wes was an absolute dream and I was amazed and impressed at just how involved he is with every aspect of his films.

Designer: Jessica Hische

Website: www.jessicahische.is

Client: Wes Anderson

SPOTLIGHT ON... LOTTA NIEMINEN

Tell us about yourself.

I'm a graphic designer, illustrator and art director living and working in New York. I'm originally from Helsinki, Finland. I studied graphic design and illustration at the University of Art and Design Helsinki and the Rhode Island School of Design, and have worked as a freelancer in both fields since 2006. After working for fashion magazine *Trendi*, Pentagram Design and RoAndCo Studio, I am now a running my own New York based studio full–time, working on a wide array of clients from various fields.

Did you always want to work as a freelancer, or did you imagine joining a design agency as a student?

It was something I had been thinking about for a while — actually, since graduation, but at that point, I wanted to work for other people so I could learn more. Working for others has been one of the best learning curves for me: you see how people run their studios, what you'd do the same or differently. You learn about how you'd want to run your own business and about the importance of collaboration. I think it also helped me understand what type of designer I aspired to be.

Ever since my first full–time designer job, I was freelancing on top of that day job. Mostly illustrations, but also graphic design projects. I got to the point where I was getting enough freelance inquiries to start turning some of them down, and after a while, it seemed like a good time to go out on my own. I felt assured that I wouldn't be short of work at least for the first couple of months, and I began to feel equipped enough to give it a shot. Honestly, I thought that if it didn't work out, I could always try to find a new full–time job. It's been over two years now, and now I really feel like I'm running a company rather than just giving a shot at freelancing.

After studying in Helsinki and New York, did you find there were different approaches to teaching design?

In Helsinki, I had an influential teacher who helped me become certain that graphic design was really what I wanted to do. There is always this uncertainty at first when choosing your career path, when you ask yourself, "Is this it?" He encouraged thinking — graphic design is not just pretty pictures, it's mostly brain work.

As a general observation, the pace at a US university was a lot faster. I noticed that although I had always thought I was a motivated and hard–working student in Helsinki, there I felt my effort only to be around average. I did eventually pick up the pace, and I feel like I learned a lot from it. My time at RISD was invaluable practice and simulation for what real–life work ended up being, whereas my studies in Helsinki — by way of fellow students and some teachers — encouraged critical thinking and artistic expression.

At Rhode Island School of Design, I focused more on illustration, which I couldn't major in at my school in Helsinki. To me, illustration was something I had been quite interested in, but I never felt like it was my strong point. I was surrounded by people who were really concentrating on illustration and were amazing at it, so I thought giving it a shot in another country would be a nice experiment — if it didn't work out, I could just forget about it. The classes at RISD were a much needed boost for my self–confidence. For the first time, I got some good, proper feedback on my illustrations. After returning from the exchange, I started doing illustration just as seriously as I was already doing graphic design.

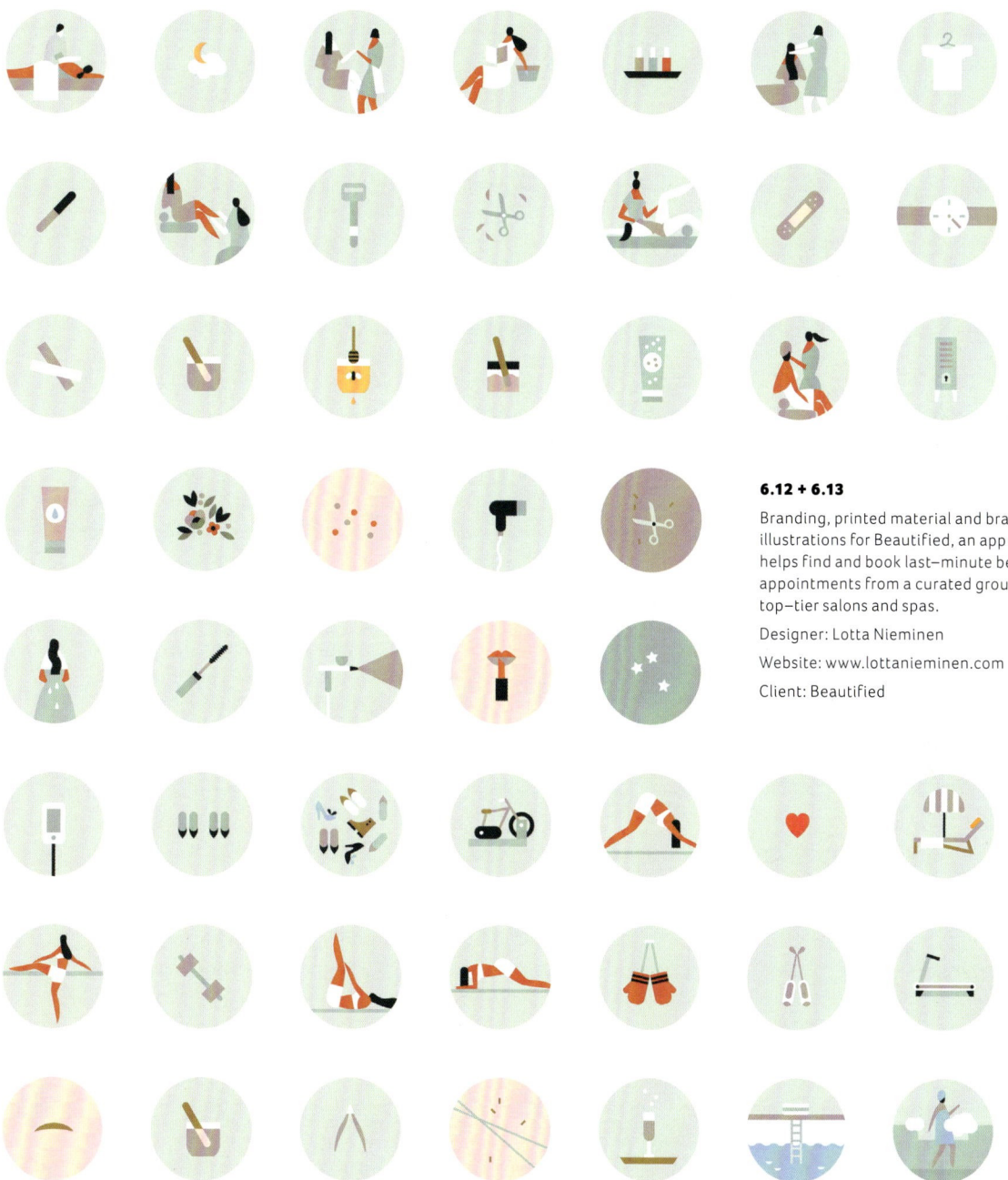

6.12 + 6.13

Branding, printed material and brand illustrations for Beautified, an app that helps find and book last-minute beauty appointments from a curated group of top-tier salons and spas.

Designer: Lotta Nieminen

Website: www.lottanieminen.com

Client: Beautified

6.12

SPOTLIGHT ON... LOTTA NIEMINEN

Do you have any tips for students and recent graduates who would like to pursue a freelance career?

For me, a great design or illustration project is one where both the client and the designer walk out of it 100% happy. If the sole purpose of a project is for the designer to get something awesome looking in their portfolio, I don't consider it a very successful project. Those goals can be reserved for personal projects, not client projects.

At the same time, if only the client leaves content and the designer feels like their creative input got drowned in all the feedback rounds, I don't think it's a very successful project either. Graphic design is about offering customer service and delivering what's commissioned, but it's also expertise and knowledge on what works best. I think that you should never give up too easily and should be prepared to back up the things you feel strongly about. Sometimes clients need a little push: they see things they haven't seen anywhere else and they're not going to necessarily digest it before understanding what they're looking at.

Learning how to argue your ideas is absolutely crucial if you want to get your visions through. Graphic design should be demystified: you should understand why a certain typeface gives the work a certain feel, and be able to explain it to the client.

Also keep your files in order. I feel like a crazy person with my almost–too–meticulously organized folders and systematically named files, but it'll go a long way when you need to find or share files later on. Especially when you start working with other people.

You have an amazing client base, how did you develop this?

What really helped me when deciding to go full–time freelance was that I had been doing it on the side of full–time jobs for quite a long time. Because of the financial safety of having a day job as a designer, I was able to freelance on only work that I thought to be truly inspiring. This helped me develop my style without a rush and build a portfolio with work I was really proud of. The kind of work you have in your portfolio is the kind of work you'll get commissioned to do, and I wanted my portfolio to give a very strong feel of what type of projects and clients I was after.

A couple of years ago, I did this personal project of a cityscape and posted it on my website. Soon after, my first building related commission came in and I've done a lot of them since. Having a profession on "both sides" has taught me a lot about that thinking too: working as a designer who commissions and as an illustrator who gets commissioned. When I'm art directing, the only thing I see is what's in someone's portfolio. It rarely crosses my mind that this person would want to do something else than what's presented on their website.

The work in your portfolio is split across graphic design and illustration. Is this for the benefit of clients, or do you take a very different approach to these types of work?

Realizing I can identify as both a graphic designer and an illustrator was a big revelation for me. When I started my graphic design studies, I built my professional identity heavily on being a designer, and it wasn't until my exchange at RISD and the positive feedback I got on my illustration work there that made me decide to pursue it as something more than a hobby on the side. Because they developed pretty separately, I think of them as very different approaches to projects. Nowadays, I feel like my professional identity is very loose: I'll wear whatever hat the project I'm working on makes me wear. Besides design and illustration I currently do art direction, photography and prop styling. For my personal motivation, I find it important not to have to be stuck to one specific discipline and way of doing. Working with illustrations is a nice change if I get designer's block with graphic design — and vice versa.

In my work, illustration and graphic design are very different, both in ways of thinking and executing. As a graphic designer, it's more about finding an answer to a question, whereas as an illustrator, I'm usually executing an answer someone else art directs. This obviously makes the two styles very different for me. I try to avoid working as both the designer and illustrator on the same project, and it's only happened a couple of times. When I design, I'd rather commission someone else to illustrate.

The type of clients I work for are different in both disciplines too. In illustration, I'm able to work for big companies as I have a set style I'm commissioned to do, but in design, I prefer working with smaller brands that I can oversee from the beginning in a more overarching way.

In graphic design my style is rather minimalist and deliberately colorful. I aim for a strong feel of space in my compositions. I also have a weakness for details and small type. Materials are very important to me, and I take great pleasure in choosing the right ones for each project. In illustrations my style is more generous, with lots of elements and details. I find it easier to play with colors and patterns in illustration than in graphic design, where my taste is more simple.

You are very active when it comes to talks, exhibitions and taking part in events. Has this helped you gain more clients and raise your profile?

I mostly do it to get a nice change from the rather solitary aspect of running a one–woman business. New clients might result of it, but I'm definitely not setting attracting new clients as a main goal when partaking in conferences or exhibitions. I do it more to explore another side of the business and the kind of work I do: I love meeting new people and these types of things also give a legitimate excuse to discuss design every once in a while. Preparing a talk is a good exercise in some serious self–analysis, and exhibitions are a nice way to explore a more artistic side of my otherwise commercial work profile.

6.13

SPOTLIGHT ON... RENA TOM AND BRYAN BOYER

Tell us a bit about yourself.

RT — Makeshift Society was born out of frustration and loneliness and a touch of stubbornness. We wanted a hybrid space that looked and felt the way that would make us the most comfortable, and informal as possible, so as not to scare off people who are unsure about organizations. Because we cater to freelancers, we are aware of the qualities they are looking for in a workplace, a meeting space, and an online organization — in short, a community for people who work alone. Managing this seeming oxymoron is what we specialize in at Makeshift.

The Makeshift Society are known for homely, beautiful spaces that make people want to work together; how important do you think environment is to a designer?

RT — Judging by the response, pretty important! Everyone has different criteria about what makes a great workspace and I don't think you can discount the "feel", especially if your profession or personal aesthetics are attuned to that naturally.

BB — It's no small thing if you're in business as a creative. If you invite your clients to a meeting and they arrive at a stale business hall, it just doesn't reflect well on you. That's not to say that things have to be glossy and clean, either. Far from it. At Makeshift Society we try to leave things just loose enough that the spaces feel genuinely lived in.

RT — Basic space planning sets up the bones of each space but then it's the soft furnishings, the art and books, and the people themselves that really create character.

You must feel very proud that so many careers have been kickstarted as a result of your work; in which areas have you seen most success and have you seen this change over time?

RT — We've actually seen people at a lot of different transition points. Some have propelled a new idea forward into a viable business, and others have simply optimized their existing career and deepened relationships with the community. We're proud that we can help our members push forward, no matter what stage they are at.

BB — Some of our favorite moments at Makeshift Society are when members find a need to work with each other. There's a lot of talk about "collaboration"

6.14

but it doesn't make any sense just for its own sake. Actually, working alone is a fantastic way to get stuff done! But when you need to do something that requires more muscle, or a wider range of skills, it's useful to have a diverse group of peers such as the community at Makeshift Society.

Working in a business support role of this type allows you to be incredibly creative, how do you maintain and develop a good overview of the current design/creative landscape?

RT — Most people don't equate business support with creativity, so that's an interesting perspective! We work with many different kinds of people, all with different goals, so our creativity is around figuring out how to best support them. It's true, though, that we probably hear about trends and themes first because we work directly and closely with the workforce. We spend a lot of time discussing the landscape and determining our place within it, and how we can possibly influence it as well.

Your spaces offer many opportunities for cross-discipline collaborations; what are the most exciting projects you've seen?

BB — We don't offer anything directly, but we make it possible for others to find collaborators. That's our role: we're the platform and the members are the ones who truly bring the opportunity, connections, and spark to make shift happen.

We've seen successful Kickstarters launch out of Makeshift Society like Lumio and Vicki Murley's CSS Animations guide. But there's not always a big tangible outcome to point to. Collaborations between people evolve as people get to know each other better. Steven Johnson talks about the "slow hunch" that great ideas emerge out of, and we see something similar happening between people as well. There's a steady stream of small interactions and discussions and then one day an opportunity emerges and boom something great happens. Our goal is to be a place where these kinds of things bubble up as a fact of being, without effort. No one likes forced collaborations.

Kickstarter was used to raise funds for your Brooklyn space; are there any tips you can offer for designers looking to crowdfund their projects?

BB — Prepare! Crowdfunding takes a lot of pre-planning and ongoing effort, so make sure that you're ready to be stressing and working while the clock is ticking down to zero.

6.14
Photograph: Bryan Boyer
Venue: Makeshift Society
Website: www.makeshiftsociety.com

6.15
Photograph: Kelli Anderson
Based in Brooklyn and San Francisco, the Makeshift Society exists to make it easier for freelancers and small teams to start and grow their businesses. As a community we learn from each other, work hard and have fun.
Venue: Makeshift Society
Website: www.makeshiftsociety.com

6.15

Starting your own agency

Starting your own design agency is a big step for any graphic designer and is a decision that could have many different reasons behind it. It could have been a goal since you were a design student, it could be that your freelance design business has been so successful and grown so much that you need to take on other staff to satisfy the demands of your clients or it could be because you are fed up working for other agencies or companies and seek the creative freedom that going out on your own provides. The ability to do the work you want to, hire a great team and work with the clients you want to is the dream of many designers. Whatever the motivation, running a business provides many challenges that need to be dealt with as well as opportunities. But before you even choose a name there are several things to consider:

- Do you have a niche/specialism and is there a need for it?

- Do you have a business plan?

- Do you have enough clients to get through the first few months?

- Will you be able to assemble a team?

- Do you have some money in the bank?

6.16

6.17

6.18

6.16 — 6.18

Agency Adpreneurs partnered with *Metro*, a newspaper that depends on brands for advertising and created The Grad Race. They ask grads to fulfill challenges set by brands using video to tell their story.

Venue: Adpreneurs

Website: www.adpreneurs.com

Client: Metro

"Try and avoid or minimize any unnecessary spending such as paying rent on a swanky studio as when you have a month when you don't make much money (and you will) your landlord will still want rent. If you can work from home then do and use a virtual office at a business center, where you can rent out desk space and meeting rooms as and when you need them."

John Gelder, Eleven Design Consultants, www.elevendesign.co.uk

Managing a design business

Running your own design business sounds very glamorous and exciting. But in reality, a design business is like any other. You still need to pay your bills and taxes on time, and generate the money to be able to do so.

Managing a design business encompasses much more than managing design projects: it encompasses managing everything! As the owner, you will find that the number of hours you will probably work during the first two years of your studio's life will increase, often considerably, as in addition to putting in a full week working on the design aspects, you will be spending a lot of time managing everything else. Time spent managing is time not spent on designing for clients, which is what generates income, so you will need to make sure that you have creative staff that you trust, and that you don't mind not working on creative things all the time.

Processes are key to managing a business. You will need to ensure that a monitoring process is in place so that work gets done on time. You will probably need a hierarchy of people who are responsible for achieving results and who are tasked with doing the work. You will need to find a process that works for you.

The bare essentials for managing a business are a calendar and planner, but as you grow and take on bigger, more complex projects that require input from a larger number of professionals you will find project management software essential. Is this in the business plan or IT

budget? If you bill by the hour, it is a good idea to record the amount of time you are spending on each project. Various software applications are available that do this easily. Remember that you are running a business, not a hobby, so you need to make sure that all of your time and progress, and that of your team, is recorded and therefore billed.

Ensuring work gets done is normally the responsibility of the studio manager and traffic/workflow team. Do you have someone who can patrol your studio and watch what is going on, who can offer help, support and encouragement when needed, and call in extra staff and skills when something out of the ordinary is required, or the design team is swamped? Or is that person you?

Schedules are critical to agree with clients so that you can manage work flow. Remember that any milestones or deadlines agreed also apply to the client. For example, if you have agreed to design a book by the end of the month, this can only be done if the client supplies the materials on time. Make sure timescales and schedules are reasonable and if work is late, communicate this to the client to ascertain how much of a problem this is. It may not be a big deal, but if it is you may need to hire some freelancers for temporary work. Tardiness does not reflect well on a service provider such as a design agency.

Marketing and promotion are also elements that a design studio will need to engage in and manage. The how–to aspect of this is

covered in Chapter 3, but as for everything else in a design studio, this will have to be planned, managed and budgeted. Marketing and promotion of a business needs to be undertaken to help achieve the aims as set out in the business plan and attract the type of clients that the studio wants. Marketing and promotion needs to focus on the spaces where such clients can be engaged with communications that highlight the strengths and USP of the studio.

Reviewing your business periodically is vitally important to assess its creative health and to gauge how well you are achieving your goals. What type of jobs and clients have you been doing? Is this different to what you aimed for in your business plan? You may find that the USP that the market sees in you is not the one you thought you had or it may mean that you are reaching out to the wrong sort of client, which could be because they pay better. Periodically reviewing your business and analyzing what you are doing will give you the information to take decisions. For example, you may be okay with the fact that the work you are doing is different to what you aimed for in your business plan, in which case carry on and look to grow this. If not, look at why you came to do this sort of work and make a concerted effort to change course. If your costs are so high that you need to take on well–paid work rather than the sort of work you want to do, get out the red pen and your budgets and look at where you can or must cut costs.

Business planning

You have to start with some idea of the work that you want to do and the particular niche you wish to inhabit. Knowing what you (and your partners) do well and knowing whether there is an audience for it should guide the type of agency that you create. Developing a business plan is an essential business tool that will guide you and help you make difficult decisions. More importantly during the business start–up stage, the process of making a business plan will force you to consider key things such as what you want to do, who your potential clients are and how you will attract them, forecast your income, estimate your costs and cash flow, budget for your expenses such as the investment in technology that you will have to make, the type of premises and number of staff, amongst other things.

A business plan typically covers five years so that you can plan for growth and have a path to follow knowing what you have to do in order to achieve your growth goals. Making a business plan will show you and others (such as a bank manager, partners or investors) whether starting a design studio is actually a viable, sustainable idea or not. Hoping that things will work out is not a business plan and starting a business without one could mean that you end with significant debts and a damaged reputation.

From the outset you will need to look at factors such as choosing directors or advisors who can share their experience and knowledge to help you make good decisions, particularly relating to things that you are not an expert on such as financial and legal aspects, and also the right structure for your company.

A business plan should be reviewed and revised annually to see how you have advanced in meeting your goals and, if you haven't, determining why. It is not a static document but a living document that will change as your business changes. If something in the plan is not working, work out why and change it for something that will work. Business and general economic conditions change which means your business plan needs to be flexible in order to embrace change. If the economy starts shrinking should you do more marketing and promotion or less? Can you postpone investment in new technology or is it essential to giving you the competitive edge that you will need to ride out a recession?

Business models

If you are forming a design studio, it will probably be a limited liability company or partnership. Your company structure will have a big effect on the way the business runs and ultimately the type of clients you work with. For example, you may choose to work with a small team and keep your practice small and boutique. However, if you plan on expanding and getting extra investment you need to structure things so that this is possible. Control of the business will be a key factor in your choice of business model. If you work with a large groups of stakeholders they may help you with initial investment and start-up money, but they will want to see a return on this and expect you to take on the clients that yield the most profit. It is important to get some advice because each type of company has different legal and taxation obligations and benefits, and whichever type of company you form, there are a range of stakeholders required by law to oversee the business such as directors, a company secretary, partners and possibly shareholders.

Top tips: Company models

If forming a company in the US you might look to models such as:

Corporation, a legal entity owned by shareholders

Partnership, a group of individuals operating together

Association, a professional body sometimes run as a not for profit

In the UK and most of Europe you may form a:

Company Limited by Guarantee, normally run by a group of directors

Company Limited by Shares, a structure governed by shareholders

Community Interest Company, a charitable or community minded company

SPOTLIGHT ON... ANNE BRASSIER

Tell us a bit about yourself.

My career in the design world started officially on 12 February 2001, at around 10am, at Airside. I am not a designer myself, but I have worked with designers in the world of design since then.

Over the ten and a half years that I was at Airside, they and I went through many different phases, evolutions and learning curves; we grew together and one helped the other. My roles have always been on the support side, from studio manager through to business development and communications, taking in production, creative direction, and creative production along the way!

There is not an obvious path between where I am now and where I was then, but there is a line through the trajectory that makes sense and one job has led to another.

You've worked with some great companies, and now you are offering creative startups the benefit of your experience — what are the main issues new design companies face?

Deciding where they fit into the creative landscape.

Sticking to their ideas whilst letting go of their ideals.

Figuring out how to wear all the different hats that small creative start ups need to wear.

Realizing that one day they may not actually be doing much actual hands–on design work if things work out...

What's guided your career progression?

Happy accidents. Or the dogged ability to see an opportunity and put myself forward for it.

My career actually started during my early years in London, in my social life. I didn't realize it then, but the people I was hanging out with and doing art projects with, were the people I would work with in the future. Many of them are now the people who are mentoring and teaching others, appearing in books, or writing their own books for that matter! They're the people that you hear on Radio 4 when they're discussing urban architecture. They have achieved incredible things and I owe much to those early friendships that have presented me with opportunities that might otherwise not have come my way. I certainly did things I wouldn't have imagined because of those friendships; nothing illegal though!

Is there a particular lesson you've learned that you wish you'd known sooner?

Honestly not really. Because in the end, I've ended up in a great place career–wise that is right for me, right now, and with a colorful résumé. However, I'm probably envious of people who know what they want to do, from what they study at college and the moment they're finished; I knew what I didn't want to do... But what I wanted was figured out along the way, step by step.

You do a lot of work helping and guiding others in the creative industry, what drives this?

A very simple feel–good factor and an inherent desire to mother people!

Airside was phenomenal for me — the directors (Nat Hunter, Alex Maclean with Fred Deakin) were supportive and nurturing to an incredible extent. As well as the amazing fun I had at Airside, I learned a huge amount and I got to work with brilliant people, doing interesting work, going to places I wanted to visit. It put me in great stead for the career that has followed.

We used to receive résumés and emails (one famous hand–scrawled fax even) begging for jobs daily. I felt sorry for some of the people sending them in — you'd be gobsmacked at how many horrific Word template résumés we received, considering they were being sent to a creative studio, asking for a creative job... So I started communicating with those people, saying — look dude, if you really want a career in design you cannot send a résumé that looks like this. It started there. I got involved in doing studio visits for students, talks at colleges and other institutions, and things like the Design Museum's Design Ventura program.

Once I left Airside, I wanted to share what I had learned. Payback for Nat, Alex and Fred's care. One big thing I learned at Airside was to work openly and collaboratively, not be secretive. Whatever information I have gathered over the 10.5 years, I will share with the younglings coming out of college and maybe spare them a mistake or two (though mistakes are good).

Could offer some "top tips" for people looking to start their own design company?

1. Ask yourself why you want to start your own venture.

Is it because you've worked elsewhere and have decided it's time to strike out on your own? Is it because you have a fantasy about the glory of running your own studio? Is it because you just want to try it? Is it because you want more control over the work you do?

Whatever the reason, it doesn't really matter, it's about identifying your motivation. As long as you have that conversation with yourself or your future colleagues, it helps sets the framework for what you want to achieve and ultimately will help dictate what kind of work you go for and the decisions you make along the way.

2. Work out what you offer, where you fit into the creative landscape, your elevator pitch.

And don't start out by trying to emulate another studio, or creative, or style of work that you admire; dig deep to think about your own vision, your own style and start there. There's nothing wrong with admiring someone and what they have achieved, and learning from it, but setting out to be the next "Studio X" is fatal.

3. Make a list of goals, wishes and dream clients.

You'll be amazed how, what seems like a pipe dream in the beginning, can become reality. Like working out what your particular offering is, working through this process helps shape where you stand, where you want to be, what you want from the whole experience. These aims can, and probably will, shift, but it's still important to start out by defining these things.

4. Answer honestly: is money a priority or not?

Money is not a dirty word. It's fine to want to make money out of being a creative. So while it shouldn't be your sole driving factor, at least acknowledge that it is important — bills must be paid, shoes must be worn!

5. Be prepared for all your plans to go out the window and change direction.

You may do so well with your studio that corporates come knocking, offering large sums of money to buy into you and your style by offering you a job. Or it may all go belly up. But at least you tried.

Or you may think you hate ad–land, then realize that you can actually make some incredibly nice work and get paid for it. It may challenge your morals...

6. Don't skimp on the finances.

I mean that in every sense. Get an accountant and practice good bookkeeping. Boring, but important.

Charge yourself out correctly. Figure out what your overheads are and salaries etc., and learn to charge clients proper, justifiable fees.

Pay yourself. Even if it's peanuts to start with.

SPOTLIGHT ON… ROGER PROCTOR, PROCTOR STEVENSON

Tell us about yourself.

When I left school I didn't really know what I wanted to do, it was something vaguely to do with art and design, as my father was a boat designer. Most of the people in the art college system wanted to be some kind of famous artist, but they didn't really know what they were getting themselves into. I was quickly told by a lecturer that I should apply for graphic design, and not really knowing what graphic design was, that's what I did.

I was very lucky I got into Bristol and then I went on a voyage of discovery. I was on a very vocational course and I worked with hot metal and letterpress. It was tactile, and it was great fun.

How did Proctor Stevenson begin?

I set up a business with someone I knew from college (that's where the Stevenson comes from) but he left after a year. Meanwhile we'd got a very lucky break with a company called Inmos, they were Britain's first semiconductor design and manufacture operation.

A great innovator called Iann Barron came up with an idea called parallel processing that allowed silicon chips to work in a parallel rather than a linear fashion. With a linear configuration, every time they performed a function there would be a disproportionate power loss. This new design addressed this issue and the concept enabled the first super computers.

My job was to build the brand for this company and the work covered the period their company grew from a team of three to when a few years later it had grown to two and a half thousand people across the UK and US with a turnover of many millions. Being totally non–technical that was a baptism by fire.

How has the company developed?

I really started here in IT branding and corporate communications and then started working in financial services as well. They are very similar markets as people that are in those industries are determined to talk to their customers in ways and terms that they can't understand. They confuse people and put up barriers, so I always worked on the basis that I was the dumbest person in the room and if they can make me understand, I can make anyone else understand it.

Over the next ten years I built the business on corporate communications design, and then in the late 1980s and early 1990s I felt that this bubble of everyone being interested in and investing in design was likely to burst. I therefore became very interested in direct marketing because it is about measurable results. It was about being able to measure success or failure of the communication and track it. Building on that I got heavily involved in direct marketing and direct mail. At one point we were one of the largest direct mail operations in the country, and we then realized that this too was going to fade we became more interested in one to one marketing. Because we were also interested in technology like Indigo variable digital print we thought there was a real opportunity with personalization. For example rather than the bland "Dear Sir" and generic communication we could personalize it in both words and image by using data such as service history, previous model choice, finance data, etc.

We then decided we weren't so much interested in that as behavior. Understanding the thing you are looking at and reacting to we started to develop technology around this. So, while we still do branding and we still do design in the conventional sense, we are much more convergent with lead tracking behavior.

How does the business operate?

At Proctors we have conventional graphic designers that work both on and offline. They work with developers, copywriters and people that work on the strategy side. It's an integrated approach.

I have always seen it as my mission to employ as many graphic designers as I can, because that is my passion. I recognize in order to create and maintain those types of jobs one has to move the goal posts all of the time and not wait for them to be moved for you; that's the reason I got involved with West of England Design Forum.

People in the creative industries are a very intelligent bunch of people and it's a broad church — that diversity interests me. What people did before they come to work here also really interests me. We have people that were designers, but we also have some that were musicians, zoologists, mathematicians and more.

From starting in Proctor Stevenson in 1979, how have you maintained currency and lasted?

I've speculated about that on a number of occasions. We have always been interested in the ideas, and we've been great opportunists. We've always tried to see how an idea can relate to what we do, and change the nature of the game.

We have this ability to take on a creative new idea and run with it. Sometimes we've spent a lot of money and resources on things we shouldn't have done, but other times we've done it and it's been a really sensible investment. Luckily we've kept moving.

I've met a lot of people from businesses that have come and gone. I know a lot of people who do really well over a short period then crash and burn; we might not have done as well as them short term, but we are still here.

How do you keep investigating and finding new things?

In my case (and I'm not sure if I'm typical), but I get my information from talking to people. I find that by talking to people, they either trigger something and I then make links between conversations with other people, or it sparks an idea that I then talk to other people about.

It's a catalytic operation and I find networking and talking to people is the way it works best for me as I'm a social person.

You are involved in a number of groups that seek to develop business and government's perception of graphic design. Do these actively inform the work you do, or is it more about giving back?

West of England Design Forum is productive in terms of getting thoughts and ideas together. I think it's a give back, but also a frustration with government and the education system.

It seems to me that education has gotten into this state of denial about graphic design being a vocational qualification. The anarchic nature of the art schools was a pretty good model. Now I'm slightly worried by the taming of it all.

Design Buddies is a really interesting project that has helped bridge the gap between education and the workplace, could you tell us more about this?

A local university used to ask people to come down to do two days worth of portfolio reviews. Many designers had to take holiday to do this which was very difficult. So we wanted to engage with students in a more productive and manageable way and get more people involved through students engaging with professionals in the designer's environment. Design Buddies was born out of that; students had the opportunity to come into a real world design environment and see what a studio was actually like.

Do you have any advice for design graduates?

Just make sure you are well connected. It's about networking, going to events, engaging and talking to people. No one is going to rock up to your door and say "here is a job" — it just doesn't happen. You need to be realistic and work damn hard.

Ethics

Companies, particularly small businesses, are often guided by the personal and professional ethics of the founder or partners. This could be a factor in determining the type of client you want to work with. For example, due to the threat of global warming, a number of pension funds are now refusing to invest in companies involved in the extraction of hydrocarbons. This is an ethical decision that you may face as hydrocarbon companies typically pay very well. You may have views on the promotion of alcohol or cigarettes or other social factors that are not compatible with certain clients. Starting out, it is hard to say no to potential clients and there will always be clients that you will immediately reject because their key product or service is morally objectionable to you. However, this gets more complicated when you start working with large companies that are subsidiaries of larger conglomerates. Other potential clients may reject working with you if they see that you have previously worked with companies that they find morally objectionable.

The *First Things First* manifesto addressed such issues as this and was published initially in 1964, and then updated in 1999 and 2014. Written by Ken Garland and first featured in *The Guardian* newspaper, the original manifesto urged designers to take a stand against consumerist culture and use their skills on pursuits that were more worthy and long-lasting. This text was updated later and signed by a new generation of designers who wished to promote the idea that graphic design is not just about selling goods, and that this view is emphasized far too prominently in publications, art schools and throughout the marketplace. Again, their wish is not that this consumerist culture is wiped out (this would not be feasible) but that designers think about wider cultural issues and use their skills more wisely.

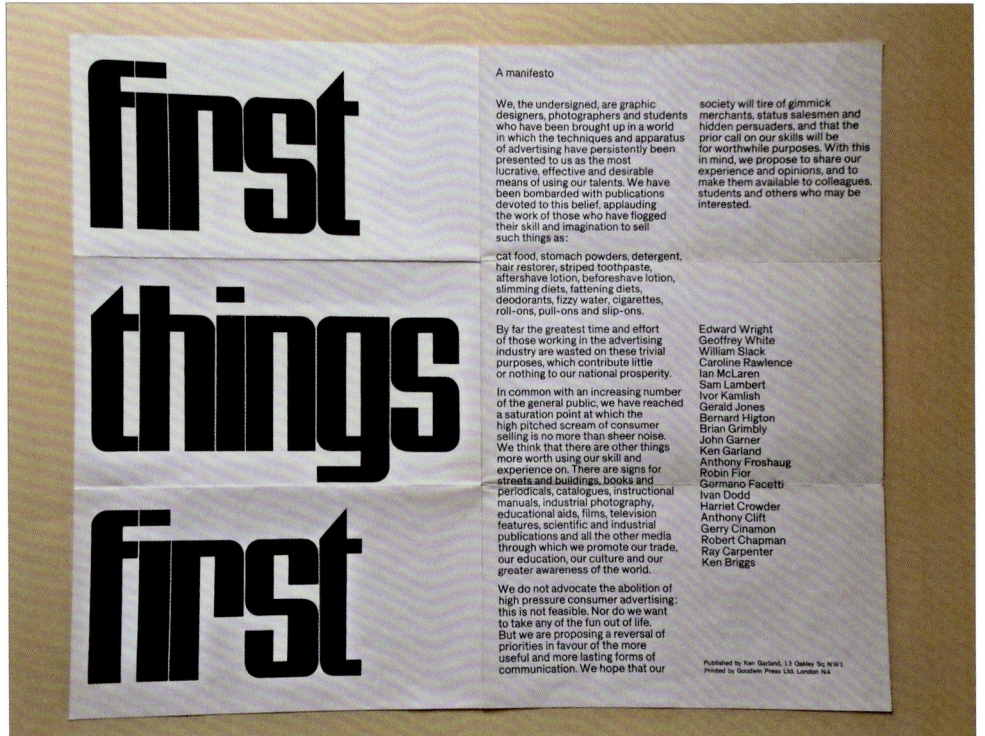

6.19

6.19

Published in 1964 and authored by Ken Garland, the *First Things First* manifesto was supported by over 400 designers. Printed in *The Guardian* newspaper it sought to radicalize an industry that had become more focused on serving capitalism rather than inspiring and helping people.

Author: Ken Garland

Website: www.kengarland.co.uk/ KG–published–writing/first–things–first/

6.20

In 1999 the original 1964 *First Things First* manifesto was updated and drew the support of an entirely new generation of graphic designers. It was published simultaneously in *Adbusters* (Canada), *Emigre* and *AIGA Journal of Graphic Design* (United States), *Eye* [pictured], *Blueprint* (Britain) and *Items* (Netherlands).

Author: Ken Garland, et al.

Website: www.eyemagazine.com/ feature/article/first–things–first–manifesto–2000

6.20

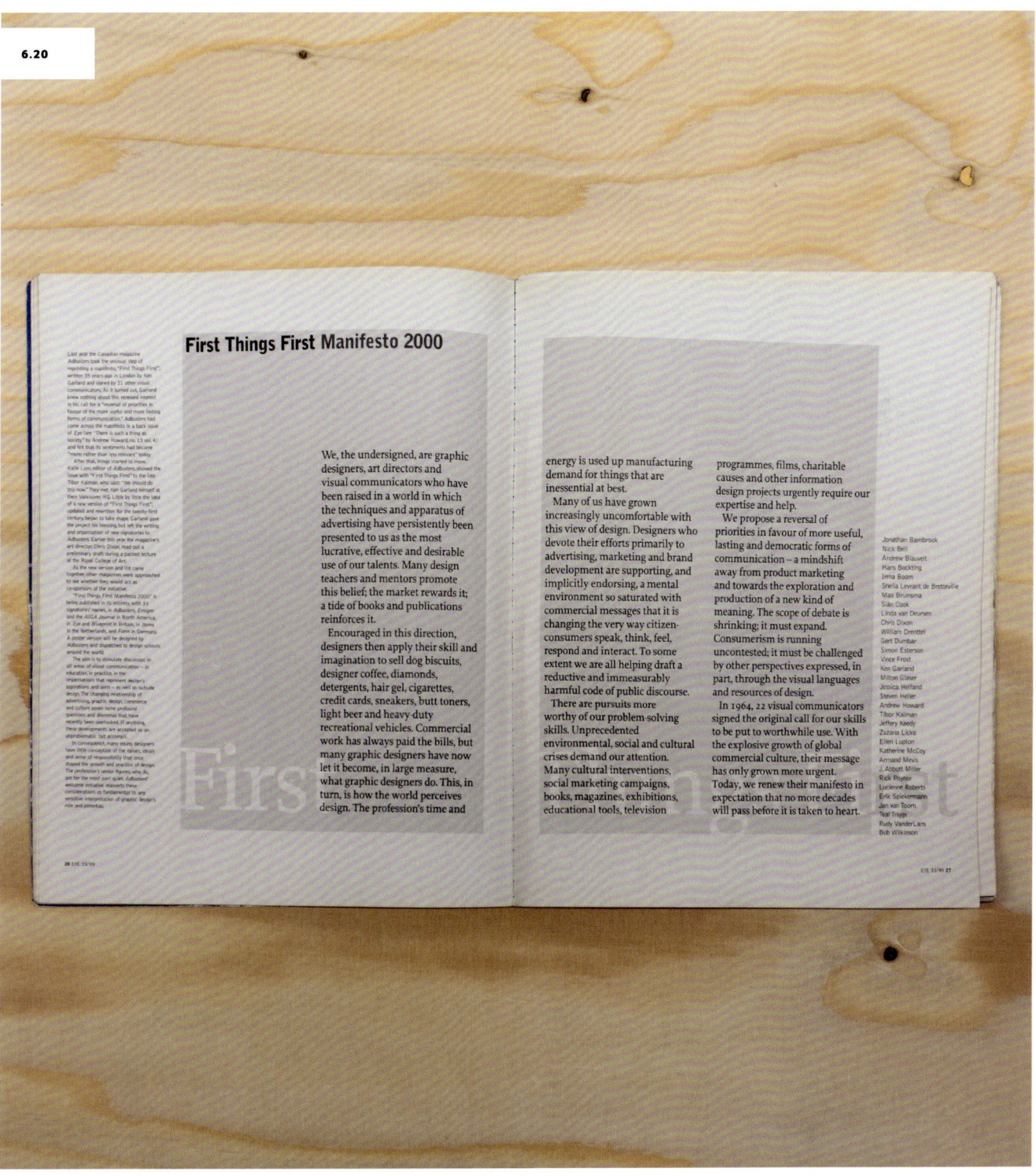

PENCIL

PENCIL

POS

- PAGE TWO -

IT'S STORY TIME

The reasons why content is
king and how you can use it to
inspire your customers to buy

STORIES FROM THE STORYTELL

- PAGES FOUR & FIVE -

SHOWCASE

Show and tell time.
A few of our favourite projects
from the Pencil portfolio

TOP T

20 years of c
boiled down
toda

Activities

7.1 — 7.3

Pencil Agency — situated in the heart of London's Soho — creates considered, bespoke content for clients across all channels but with a particular love of print. With this in mind it would only seem right that Pencil promoted itself and the importance of curated content to brands by way of a beautifully designed newspaper. Printed in navy and fluorescent orange inks, and delivered in matching envelope, *Pencil Post* was designed to really stand out on the desks of those it was sent to. The newspaper was delivered to select current and potential clients, complete with hand-written personalized message from Pencil Agency's Creative Director — Jenny Dyson.

Pencil Post was exceptionally well received by recipients, fully realizing the brief (of promoting Pencil Agency) and resulting directly in new business. An added sense of achievement came from the attention generated online by the project and the praise received by the international design community.

Designer: Chloë Galea

Website: www.chloegalea.com

Creative Director: Jenny Dyson

Studio: Pencil Agency

ACTIVITY 1: YOUR PROFILE

Compile 400 words for an "About Me" section on your website.

A clear, consistent identity will help potential clients decide whether you are the right person to work on their project. The risk of taking on a designer (or design company) can be very high, so you need to use the right language to demonstrate that you are the right choice. This text can be used in a number of places such as pages on your website, résumé, tender documents, and more. It can also be further edited for social media bios, and even the "additional information" sections on job applications.

Think of yourself objectively as a brand, and use your 'story' to make this as unique and clear as possible. Remember the text needs to carry all of the keywords that people may search for. The bullet points opposite might help might help to prompt information you might have forgotten to include.

Basic information

- Name

- Contact information

- Exactly what do you do?

- How can you help people?

- Where can your work be seen?

- What else do you do?

Expertise

- What are your key design skills?

- What is your design passion?

- Are there skills you'd like to develop and learn?

- Where did you learn these skills?

- Where, and how, can people see proof of these skills?

- How are you different to the competition?

- What can you offer beyond design skills? (Language skills, copywriting, web skills, etc.)

Publicity

- Do you have any testimonials?

- Have you received any (good) press?

- Do you blog or use social media?

- Has anyone posted nice things about you on their blog or website?

Location

- Where are the places you've worked and lived?

- Where are you currently located?

- How far would you commute for work and/or what areas do you cover?

- Where would you most like to live and work?

- Are you able to speak more then one language, and if so at what level (basic, conversational, fluent)?

Experience

- How long have you worked as a designer?

- How many years have you spent training?

- Have you won any awards or competitions?

Edit and structure

Once you have all this information together, edit it down. Only use the bits that demonstrate how great you are and make you sound like an interesting, employable person.

ACTIVITY 2: YOUR RÉSUMÉ

Compile a résumé for one of the following job adverts:

Freelance Graphic Design, Digital Branding Agency

Versatile freelance designers and artworkers needed on an ad hoc basis to join an established, full–service agency. Working closely with a talented team, you'll provide a true variety of integrated campaigns and creative marketing communication materials to many leading brands and retailers.

Integral skills for the role are:
Integrated campaigns, POS, brochure, print experience
Exposure to retail brands
Good commercial awareness
Good communicator
Ability to work solo on projects but also a solid team player
To work under pressure and to tight deadlines
Good presentation skills
End–to–end designer — concept to artwork

Graphic Designer, Publishing and Events

As this role is predominantly print-based, excellent InDesign and typographic skills are essential, while Photoshop and Illustrator skills are desirable. Working alongside the Head of Design and closely with the editorial team, you should be a confident decision-maker and communicator, able to demonstrate concepts quickly and effectively. A calm and organised demeanour is vital as the role will involve working on multiple projects simultaneously. An interest in publishing and events would obviously be advantageous. You must have a degree-level qualification in Graphic Design or similar, and if invited for interview you must be able to demonstrate your suitability for the role through the print work in their portfolio.

One of the most important points to remember when compiling a résumé is that this will often be the first that a potential employer sees of you. So it's important that the tone of voice and design are thoroughly considered and an accurate reflection of you.

Use the following pointers to help.

Personal information

Make sure that you include up-to-date contact information at the top of the first (and perhaps every) page. Use a professional-sounding email address, and if you include a phone number (and you should), make sure you answer it in a professional manner from this point onwards.

Profile

This can be a useful section to include, as résumés can be dry if they are just lists and bullet points.

With a good profile section you can tell your story and show more of your personality. Remember to keep it brief though. It should be no longer than three sentences.

Experience

Where have you worked, and what was your role(s)?

What were your day-to-day duties and responsibilities?

Can you highlight any achievements?

What clients did you work with there?

Did you use any specific processes, techniques and/or tools?

Education

Where did you study?

What courses did you take, and what were the results?

Are there any specific achievements you can highlight?

References

It is usual to have two or three references ready when you are applying for a job. You can include their details, or simply state that references are available upon request.

Other possible sections

Shows and exhibitions: have you exhibited your work anywhere?

Awards: have you won any student/industry awards?

Hobbies: list a few pursuits here that show you are a well-rounded person and a few more that relate to the discipline.

Languages: this can be great if you are applying for work with a multinational company.

Last note

Always list positive attributes — never include things that you aren't very good at. It's okay to say you are still learning, but avoid words like beginner, or amateur.

Never mention something that you won't be able to back up. You will need to give concrete examples in an interview so always use this as a test when deciding what to include on your résumé.

A very last note

Keep it simple.

ACTIVITY 3: STRUCTURING YOUR PORTFOLIO

Put together a portfolio of your best work to date.

Much like a résumé, clients and employers may see your portfolio a long time before they meet you. A good portfolio will be professional, easy to navigate, consistent and should show off your skills and personality.

Whether your portfolio is printed or online, the same rules and layout guides can be adopted and it is good to link the two as this can help you achieve a more coherent presence.

Project captions

- Do you have a clear convention for titling projects?

- What is the project?

- What was the project objective, and how did you meet this?

- What materials and processes did you use?

- Would the client offer a testimonial?

- Is there a web link for people to see more?

Suggested layouts

ACTIVITY 4: INTERVIEW SKILLS

Ask a friend/colleague/mentor or professor to run you through a practice interview.

For senior positions you can expect a formal, traditional interview, but for many junior roles you will be invited in for a chat and a run through your portfolio. While a chat is a far less formal situation, it is good to be prepared and have some answers ready for the type of questions you are likely to be asked.

Most questions for design roles will be about your portfolio. The interviewer will ask about inspirations, technical abilities, experience and also try to establish your part in the project if you are presenting group work or pieces developed while in education. When discussing your portfolio have something positive to say about every project (you shouldn't have work you don't like in there) and make sure this comment links to the job role: if they have asked for specific skills, ensure these are covered somewhere, even if you need to generate a new piece of work.

Discussing your work

Always say "I" more than "we" as they are interested in you, and you need to take responsibility for your work and choices.

Answering the question

Why do you want this job?

What do you like about the company?

Has their work inspired you?

When asked why you want to the job talk about your aspirations, and also talk about how you can achieve these by taking on the role.

Research the company and understand their clients, ethos and processes, and then make clear how you will fit in.

Where do you see yourself in five years?

What jobs can you move on to?

When asked about your future aspirations, be positive and realistic. If you are going for a junior position it's great to say that you would like to move into a more senior as this shows ambition.

When you express these ambitions, make sure to voice them in the context of the company you are speaking too. Even if you know you are taking on the role to gain experience, you need to express the desire to grow within the company as they are investing in you from the moment they take you on.

ACTIVITY 5: DRAWING UP A CONTRACT

Draw up a list of all the aspects you will need to write into a contract for the following job:

A two-sided, full-color, half-letter/A6 flyer with full bleed. You will need to supply final artwork in the form of a PDF. The client will supply copy, images, logos and brand guidelines. The initial print run will be 5,000 copies.

Think about the questions you'll need to ask the client, do you need any further information?

Use the prompts below to ensure that your contract covers all the details you need to help keep the project on schedule and within budget.

What do you understand the brief to be?

What information do you need before you begin?

How long do you think this will take you to design?

How many amend stages are you going to offer?

What are the specific things you are going to deliver (perhaps reiterate the client's brief)?

Who is responsible for printing?

Who will generate/approve the print spec?

Essential information to include

Costs (with calculations if by hour or section)

Dates (start, interim and delivery)

Deliverables listed in detail

Responsibilities of the designer and client

Payment details

ACTIVITY 6: DRAWING UP AN INVOICE

Generate an invoice for the job outlined in Activity 5.

You'll usually invoice for work on completion, but it is useful to refer back to the brief to ensure that the client fully appreciates that the job has been completed to the agreed specification.

Essential information to include

Your contact details

Date

The name of the client (a contact name is good if you are working with a specific person).

Agreed commission: briefly reiterate the brief and highlight the exact deliverables: what you are going to make. Clearly state what you are invoicing for (is it on completion of the work, or a stage of the work?).

Payment: clearly state how much you are invoicing for and how this should be paid. Make sure you include clear payment instructions for the client, and how soon you wish to be paid from the invoicing date (this is normally 28 days).

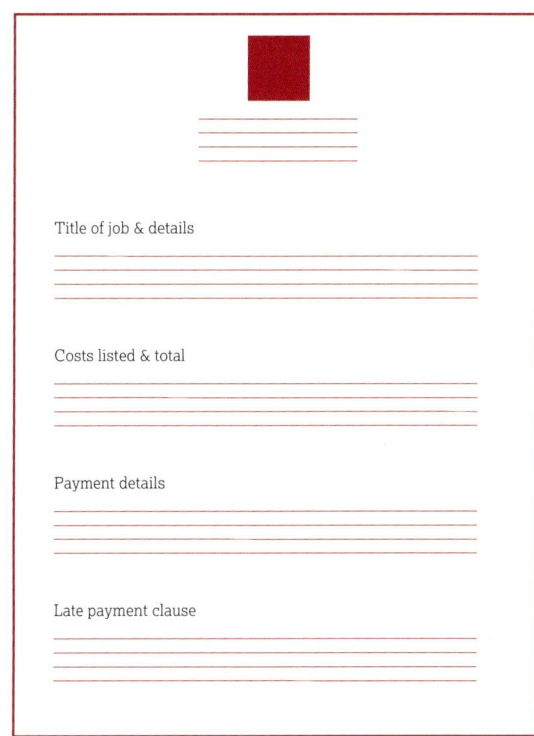

Title of job & details

Costs listed & total

Payment details

Late payment clause

8.1

8.2

MAP
Route taken

Appendix

NORWIC

8.1 — 8.3
A conceptual piece that looks at the way information is consumed and subverts it. Unassuming people were photographed in Norwich, cropped so that they become solitary figures.

Designer: Redwan El–Harrak

Website: www.r–elharrak.co.uk

Technical tips

Files

Always keep a backup of files as clients are not often understanding when it comes to lost work.

Work in the correct color space from the outset as converting from RGB (for web) to CMYK (for print) will affect the artwork and can create undesirable, muddy outcomes.

Try to maintain some order to make sure you can find things easily: most designers work with a simple system of one folder per client, and then sub–folders for each project. You may also label these folders with job numbers that correspond to invoicing references.

When it comes time to hand over deliverables you should discuss how the original artwork files will be handled. Many clients will expect to be given these, but unless they specifically ask for them (or full copyright) in the first instance, then you are not obligated to hand over anything more than the final documents.

If you did hand over all of the files to the client this could affect your on–going work — they could hand your work to a cheaper junior when it comes time for updates and you will miss out.

Sizes

Generally size will be determined by the type of project you are working on, but some good rules to follow are:

Never work at less than 100%

If you are working on a web project, but suspect files will be used in other forms at a later date, treat it like a print project and scale down the necessary files when you are ready to upload

Artwork delivery

As previously mentioned, negotiate early on what files will be handed over at the start of the job. If you are working with a third party it is equally important that you speak to them. Some printers have a preference for particular PDF versions, and many web developers like PSD mock–ups to be delivered in a specific way.

Always check sizes in the early stages, and make sure you have understood any special requirements like special printing processes or Pantone colors. If you miss things early on, corrections will add time to the end of the job and the client will not pay for this.

Bleed and crop marks

Bleed and crop marks are essential to the print process for registration and trimming. If you forget them, your design work will either be manually adjusted by the printer on the press, or refused entirely. This can be an embarrassing thing to explain to a client…

Check the bleed required by your printer.

Depending on the type of printer used, you may have to supply documents set up in different ways. Some machines will add crop marks to your artwork, and if you have added them manually, it can confuse things.

Archiving

Always back up work twice, and then once more for luck. Keeping a good archive is very easy to do with Time Machine on Macs, and cloud services like Google Drive and Dropbox. There's no reason work should ever be lost and it is vital that all versions of live projects are backed up regularly as clients won't pay for the time it takes to re–do lost pieces.

Once a project is delivered it is a good idea to keep an archive of the final pieces on a cloud service and/or hard drive (perhaps zip up some preparatory work as this can come in useful in future). Clearly label everything so it can be found when the client returns for an update and include all assets supplied by the client (logos, etc.).

Licensing & Copyright

When negotiating a price it is important that you understand the licensing and copyright implications. If the client wishes to own the full copyright to a final piece this will mean two things: you will not be able to claim any future ownership or use (putting the work in your portfolio for example) and you can normally charge more as the client is buying the work and full ownership.

Licensing will normally apply to campaigns and image–based work. If you are commissioned to create a poster for the London Underground, you will set your price accordingly. If further down the line the client wishes to use the work on train station platforms too, then you may be able to negotiate a fee for the extended license.

You will need to be very clear about licensing and copyright when writing your contracts and often have to explain the terms to your client as many will think by commissioning you, they will own the outcomes outright, and this is not the case unless it is stated clearly.

Color and DPI

RGB is used for any outcomes that utilize projected light: projections, film, websites, etc.

CMYK is used for any print projects.

Special and spot colors may be printed in addition to CMYK, but this is normally costly and only used when a client needs a very specific hue or effect.

Print files should be sized at 300dpi and at 100% (TIFF files are still a safe choice).

Web files are traditionally sized at 72ppi but retina screens require 144ppi, so create files for both dimensions (again, working at 100%).

When saving for the web JPGs will work well for photographs; GIFs are good for logotypes and short animations; PNGs offer great results for photographs and logotypes.

Other

All designers have their own methods of organization and systems that help them stay organized and keep the creative juices flowing. Here are a few tips that might help you:

Take regular beaks, as tired eyes don't see detail.

Know what the brief is asking of you before you start.

Do your research.

Test your design work.

Maintain a tidy and organized desk space, or things get lost.

If you are messy, clear up before you go home at night, no matter how late.

To stay inspired, make time to get out and look at things.

Measure twice, cut once.

Never forget the end user: you are designing for people.

Remember, it's only a job.

A guide to finances

Working for yourself, or setting up your own agency, will require some knowledge of finance and it's certainly beyond the scope of this book to provide extensive financial advice. However, the following discussions are worth bearing in mind.

And remember, bringing in professional help can alleviate potential problems: a good accountant will save you money in the long run in addition to helping give you greater control over your business.

Freelance finances

You are in business to make money, right? Making money is about maximizing your income but also minimizing your expenses. Every company needs to keep an eye on the finances, but for a freelancer this is especially important, as you are the sole person bringing in money. For most creative people dealing with finances is not a natural skill and can cause real stress. The best advice is to be disciplined about organizing yourself from the beginning and proactively learn the basics. Setting budgets, and sticking to them, will help you manage your finances and be profitable. If receipts and invoices are left to mount up, bookkeeping will become an unmanageable task so get a system in place to organize this and keep and update financial records as you go along. Record keeping will give you an understanding of your expenses and help you set realistic budgets, which in turn will help you fix rates for your work that will enable you to make money. Your earning capacity will also inform the level of expenses that your business can support.

There are many things you will have to purchase for your work that you can claim back against tax, and various ways that you can pay yourself that are tax efficient. If you aren't willing to ask for help, finances can become a demanding and unforgiving beast, particularly when the tax man is not happy. Taking the time to become more knowledgeable and familiar with things like budgets, costs, book keeping and taxes will stand you in good stead for the future and provide a foundation upon which your business can grow and thrive.

Freelance rates

Design is not a hobby and so you have to get used to talking about money and discussing your rates, which is the market value of your work. You should never feel awkward or embarrassed asking for money in exchange for work. Every job takes time and this needs to be paid for.

Determining your rates does not have to be a difficult process, but you have to get them right if you are to win clients, make a living and survive. Start by considering how many hours or days a week you will be able to charge for. This is always less than you might think. Unless you work weekends, you will never design five days a week as you are likely to spend one day a week on administration and perhaps another attending meetings. Chasing work also takes a lot of time. Beyond this, you will need to set time aside to refresh your portfolio, update social media accounts and other business-related tasks. Any time you spend doing business-related activities, even if not directly working on a client brief, needs to be factored into your rate structure.

One method to calculate your rates is to start by looking at how much you would like to earn over the course of the year, bearing in mind that at least 30% of this will be spent on taxes, insurance and other business expenses. Once you have your yearly figure, divide this by 10 months (setting aside a few weeks for holidays, illness, etc.) and then by the average number of days you expect to work on client projects (likely three days a week). This will give you your day rate.

You may also want to look at a week and month rate if you are freelancing in-house and designing five days a week. This rate will typically be less than five times your day rate as your rate won't be covering time spent on meetings or other general business activities.

Feedback from potential clients and other designers will give you an idea of the range of rates that the market is willing to pay, which will allow you to adjust yours.

Apart from taxes, there are many other costs that you will need to take into account when setting your rates. You may also need to factor in health care or national insurance/social security, or insurance to cover periods when you are unable to work due to ill health and even liability insurance in case you run into legal problems with clients and general insurance for the equipment you use in your day–to–day business. If your computer breaks you will need to replace it fast! A pension is another expense that is often not considered until much later, but if you want to have a comfortable retirement then you need to start planning for that and set aside part of what you earn on a regular basis.

Having competitive rates is important, but don't undervalue yourself. You have to pay your bills and have some money to enjoy life. You may choose to discount your rate, but don't let a client push you to charge less. Conversely, if your rates are high potential clients may baulk at them. If you find this is the case, look at why your rates seem high to clients. Have you based your rates on those of very successful peers or design agencies or do you have high costs?

Agency finances

Although dealing with numbers may not be the most exciting part of running your business, remember that numbers are your friends and managing them well will help you be successful.

Cash flow is king and what keeps a business alive. It doesn't matter if you have $20,000 of invoices out if you cannot pay the rent. It is important to learn basic accounting and budgeting skills so that you can manage the financial side of running your own business, keep records and be organized. Invoicing, paying taxes and other financial tasks are much easier and quicker if your information is well organized. If you can afford it, hire someone to do your bookkeeping. As you grow, a good accountant will save you more money in the long term than you pay them to look after the books, plus it will allow you to focus your time on billable work.

Budgeting is important as beyond the money you need to live on you will always have business costs and overheads to cover. Do you want to miss a pitch meeting because you ran out of cash and couldn't buy a train ticket? Paying the wages of your employees should always be a priority as a business cannot survive without its workers. In addition to established full–time staff, you may also have invoices from freelancers and collaborators who rely on you and who you need, so treat them well.

If you develop a reputation for late payment, freelancers may decide not to work with you. Utility bills are next on the list, and this can range from heating and rent to insurance and accountant's fees.

Every business needs money to invest in growth and expansion. As new technology and software is released you will need to invest so that you don't fall behind your competitors or appear out of date. You should have a budget for this and stick to your budget. You don't need every new software release or new piece of technology. Invest in those things that will help you achieve your business plan, and again, stick to your budget.

As you expand, the range of things you will need to finance will increase, such as larger offices, a marketing budget so that more and bigger clients know that you exist, greater expenditure on technology, as well as a contingency fund to deal with unforeseen costs such as bringing in freelance help when you are overstretched or buying a bit of kit that is absolutely essential to complete a high–paying job. It is also prudent to develop a good relationship with your bank manager and talk through your business plan with him or her so that an overdraft or loan may be readily available to cover a short–term cash flow problem. Always try to plan ahead for what you will need for where you might be in a few years.

Agency quotes

Every design firm has rates they charge for work, which are determined by its cost structure and the value it places on its work. Projects are typically quoted for based on an hourly rate and an estimation of the time it will take to complete a job, or an overall project price that factors in the amount of work it will take plus a profit margin. It is good practice to keep track of prevailing market rates so that you are not under- or over-charging.

Clients like to know exactly what they are getting from you and you should communicate this to them in the quotation in the clearest possible terms: for example, a full-color book with a certain number of pages, cover and illustrations.

To provide a competitive quote that will enable you to make money requires you to assess exactly what is required to complete a job, the time it will take and the resources that you will need to use in order to do so. If you under quote, you will lose money as very few clients are prepared to pay for your oversights. At a bare minimum, calculate roughly how many hours you think a job might take and then apply either your hourly, daily or weekly rate. You may factor in the ability to pay of each client and adjust accordingly. If your client is a small business, you could be more precise in your calculations to provide a tighter or even a

discounted price. Conversely, with a larger client that could receive a great deal of value from your work, you may choose to include a higher margin.

When a client calls, do not feel pressured to give an instant quote. Provide a ballpark range and say that you will send a quotation through once you have properly analyzed what the job entails. It is common practice for negotiation on price to occur so you may choose to start with a higher quote with the expectation that you will be negotiated down by the client. Remember, that it is very hard to start low and ask for the fee to be increased once you realize that you will not make any money from a project. You should know your cost structure and what your break-even price is. Stick to your absolute limits in terms of price and margin and if the client is looking to do a job too cheaply, you can refuse to take the job on. However, as a general rule negotiation is a good thing, as it means the client wants to work with you but needs to find an affordable way to do so.

Any quote should include the direct costs for the purchase of fonts, equipment or other professional services that are vital to the project and these should be itemized. Remember that your rates will also have to take into account the fact that you will need to replace and upgrade your business equipment from time to time, and that you have other indirect business costs to cover such as rent, utilities and insurance.

Invoicing

Whether you are a freelancer or run your own business, you will need to invoice clients in order to get paid. Invoicing is an essential part of the business process as both you and your client will need a paper trail to track income and expenditure, run your businesses and pay your taxes. Create a process for invoicing that works for you. Do you bill after the completion of each job or do you do it each week or even each month?

Sending an invoice indicates that a project, or part of it, has concluded successfully. Always ask a client to acknowledge the receipt of an invoice either by signing for it or sending an email confirmation. This will ensure you've drawn attention to it as well as starting the clock ticking if your client is slow in paying. No matter how much a client chases you for progress of a project, most will drag their feet when it comes to paying you, so be prompt when invoicing and chase payments.

The more payment options you can offer, the more likely it is the client will pay swiftly. Most designers will accept cash, checks or direct bank transfers, but you could also consider online systems.

A guide to contracts

Contracts

An acceptance of commission form should be supplied to your client for each commission should you not receive an equivalent. The text supplied here should be sufficient for most commissions. However, note that in particular, picture book contracts, which will be supplied by the publisher, involve additional clauses relating to royalties, co–edition agreements and subsidiary rights, such as translation and merchandising rights.

ACCEPTANCE OF COMMISSION

To:
For your commission for artwork as follows:
Title/Subject:
Commissioned by:
Delivery dates:
Fee: £/$
Expenses: £/$

Special terms (if any):

The Standard Terms and Conditions for this commission and for the later licensing of any rights are shown on the back of this page. Please review them together with the above and let me know immediately if you have any objection or queries. Otherwise it will be understood that you have accepted them.

THIS COMMISSION IS SUBJECT TO ALL THE FOLLOWING TERMS AND CONDITIONS

Signature of designer:
Date:

Sample terms and conditions

Payment
The Client shall pay all invoices within 30 days of their receipt.

Cancellation
If a commission is cancelled by the Client, the Client shall pay a cancellation fee as follows:

i.   25%of the agreed fee if the commission is cancelled before delivery of roughs;
ii.   33% of the agreed fee if the commission is cancelled at the rough stage;
iii. 100% of the agreed fee if the commission is cancelled on the delivery of artwork;
iv.   pro rata if the commission is cancelled at an intermediate stage.

In the event of cancellation, ownership of all rights granted under this Agreement shall revert to the Designer unless the artwork is based on the Client's visual or otherwise agreed.

Delivery

The Designer shall use her/his best endeavors to deliver the artwork to the Client by the agreed date and shall notify the Client of any anticipated delay at the first opportunity in which case the Client may (unless the delay is the fault of the Client) make time of the essence and cancel the commission without payment in the event of the Designer failing to meet the agreed date.

The Client shall make an immediate objection upon delivery if the artwork is not in accordance with the brief. If such objection is not received by the Designer within 21 days of delivery of artwork it shall be conclusively presumed that the artwork is acceptable.

Approval/Rejection

Should the artwork fail to satisfy, the Client may reject the artwork upon payment of a rejection fee as follows:

i.   25% of the agreed fee if the artwork is rejected at the rough stage.

ii.   50% of the agreed fee if the artwork is rejected on delivery.

In the event of rejection, ownership of all rights granted under this Agreement shall revert to the Designer unless the artwork is based on the Client's visual or otherwise agreed.

Changes

If the Client changes the brief and requires subsequent changes, additions or variations, the Designer may require additional consideration for such work. The Designer may refuse to carry out changes, additions or variations which substantially change the nature of the commission.

Further reading

Ethics

Roberts, L. (2006), *Good: An Introduction to Ethics in Graphic Design*, AVA Publishing.

Portfolio & résumé

Macnab, M. (2008), *Decoding Design: Understanding and Using Symbols in Visual Communication*, How Design Books.

Stone, T. (2010), *Managing the Design Process, Volume 1: Concept Development*, Rockport.

Taylor, F. (2013), *How to Create a Portfolio & Get Hired: A Guide for Graphic Designers & Illustrators*, Laurence King.

Wheeler, A. (2009), *Designing Brand Identity: An Essential Guide for the Whole Branding Team, 3rd Edition*, John Wiley & Sons, Ltd.

Business

Airey, D. (2012), *Work for Money, Design for Love: Answers to the Most Frequently Asked Questions About Starting and Running a Successful Design Business (Voices That Matter)*, New Riders.

Arden, P. (2003), *It's Not How Good You Are, It's How Good You Want To Be*, Phaidon Press.

Davies, J. & Brazell, D. (2013), *Becoming a Successful Illustrator*, Fairchild Books.

de Soto, D. (2014), *Know Your Onions: Graphic Design: How to Think Like a Creative, Act Like a Businessman and Design Like a God*, Bis Publishers.

de Soto, D. (2014), *Know Your Onions: Web Design: Jet Propel Yourself into the Driving Seat of a Top-Class Web Designer and Hurtle towards Creative Stardom*, Bis Publishers.

de Soto, D. (2014), *What to Put in Your Portfolio and Get a Job: Graphic Design*, Articul8 Publishing.

Glei, J. K. & 99U (2013), *Manage Your Day-to-Day: Build Your Routine, Find Your Focus, and Sharpen Your Creative Mind (The 99U Book Series)*, Amazon Publishing.

Glei, J. K. & 99U (2013), *Maximize Your Potential: Grow Your Expertise, Take Bold Risks & Build an Incredible Career (The 99U Book Series)*, Amazon Publishing.

Glei, J. K. & 99U (2014), *Make Your Mark: The Creative's Guide to Building a Business with Impact (The 99U Book Series)*, Amazon Publishing.

Moross, K. (2014), *Make Your Own Luck: A DIY Attitude to Graphic Design and Illustration*, Prestel.

NESTA (Editor) (2011), *Launch Your Own Successful Creative Business: Creative Enterprise Toolkit, 3rd Revised Edition*, NESTA.

(See also: www.nesta.org.uk/publications/creative-enterprise-toolkit)

Olins, W. (2008), *Wally Olins: The Brand Handbook, 1st edition*, Thames & Hudson.

Shaughnessy, A. (2012), *How to be a Graphic Designer, Without Losing Your Soul, 2nd edition*, Laurence King.

Shaughnessy, A. & Brook, T. (2009), *Studio Culture: The Secret Life of the Graphic Design Studio*, Unit Editions.

Stone, T. (2010), *Managing the Design Process, Volume 1: Concept Development*, Rockport.

Ideas

Ambrose, G. & Aono-Billson, N. (2010), *Basics Graphic Design 01: Approach and Language*, AVA Publishing.

Armstrong, H. (2009), *Graphic Design Theory: Readings from the Field*, Princeton Architectural Press.

Barnard, M. (2005), *Graphic Design as Communication*, Routledge.

Barry, P. (2008), *The Advertising Concept Book: Think Now, Design Later*, Thames & Hudson.

Bergström, B. (2009), *Essentials of Visual Communication*, Laurence King.

Burtenshaw, K. et al. (2006), *The Fundamentals of Creative Advertising*, AVA Publishing.

Chandler, D. (2007), *Semiotics: The Basics*. Routledge.

Clarke, M. (2007), *Verbalising the Visual: Translating Art and Design into Words*, AVA Publishing.

Crow, D. (2010), *Visible Signs: An Introduction to Semiotics in the Visual Arts, 2nd edition,* AVA Publishing.

Heller, S. & Vienne, V. (2012), *100 Ideas that Changed Graphic Design,* Laurence King.

Ingledew, J. (2011), *The A - Z of Visual Ideas: How to Solve any Creative Brief,* Laurence King.

Johnson, B. (2014), *Design School Wisdom,* Chronicle Books.

Kress, G. Van Leeuwen, T. (1996), *Reading Images: The Grammar of Visual Design,* Routledge.

Leonard, N. & Ambrose G. (2012), *Basics Graphic Design 02: Design Research: Investigation for successful creative solutions,* AVA Publishing.

Leonard, N. & Ambrose G. (2012), *Basics Graphic Design 03: Idea Generation,* AVA Publishing.

Lupton, E. (2011), *Graphic Design Thinking: Beyond Brainstorming (Design Briefs),* Princeton Architectural Press

Lupton, E. & Cole Phillips, J. (2008) *Graphic Design: The New Basics,* Princeton Architectural Press.

Noble, I. & Bestley, R. (2011), *Visual Research: An Introduction to Research Methodologies in Graphic Design,* AVA Publishing.

Poynor, R. (2003), *No more rules: Graphic Design and Postmodernism,* Laurence King.

Sagmeister, S. & Hall, P. (2009), *Sagmeister: Made You Look,* Harry N. Abrams, Inc.

Sagmeister, S. Nettle, D. & Heller, S. (2013), *Things I Have Learned in My Life So Far, Updated Edition,* Harry N. Abrams, Inc.

Wigan, M. (2006), *Basics Illustration: Thinking Visually,* AVA Publishing.

Skills

Ambrose, G. & Harris P. (2008), *The Fundamentals of Graphic Design,* AVA Publishing.

Cleaver, P. (2014), *What they didn't teach you in design school: What you actually need to know to make a success in the industry,* Ilex Press.

Cullen, K. (2007), *Layout Workbook: A Real-world Guide to Building Pages in Graphic Design,* Rockport Publishers Inc.

Gatter, G. (2010), *Production for Print, 2nd Revised edition,* Laurence King.

Knight, C. & Glaser, J. (2010), *The Graphic Design Exercise Book,* Rotovision.

Marshall, L. & Meachem, L. (2012), *How to Use Type,* Laurence King.

Squire, V. (2006), *Getting it Right with Type: The Do's and Don'ts of Typography,* Laurence King

Inspiration

Heller S. & Talarico L. (2010), *Graphic: Inside the Sketchbooks of the World's Great Graphic Designers,* Thames & Hudson.

Heller, S. & Talarico L. (2011), *Typography Sketchbooks,* Thames & Hudson.

Fletcher, A. (2001), *The Art of Looking Sideways,* Phaidon Press Ltd.

Fletcher, P. (2006), *Picturing and Poeting,* Phaidon Press Ltd.

Acknowledgments

The author would like to thank Sarah, Mary, Phil and Rachel Leonard, Katie and Manuel Cruz, Lesley Ripley, Leafy Cummins, Paul Allen, Alex Bradbeer, Rich Hurst, Jamie Homer, Matt Corvis, Caroline Herdman-Grant and Gavin Ambrose for their support and encouragement.

The author would also like to thank Paul Harris for his contributions and all of the students I have worked with for inspiring this text.

Thank you also to all who contributed to this book and offered your valuable time, help, insight and advice.

The view from Lucania is an independent organization founded by Stefano Tripodi in 2010. We support South of Italy through the implementation of audiovisual concepts, exhibitions, events, workshops, productions related to photography and cinema, overseen by international photographers and directors.

theviewfromlucania.com

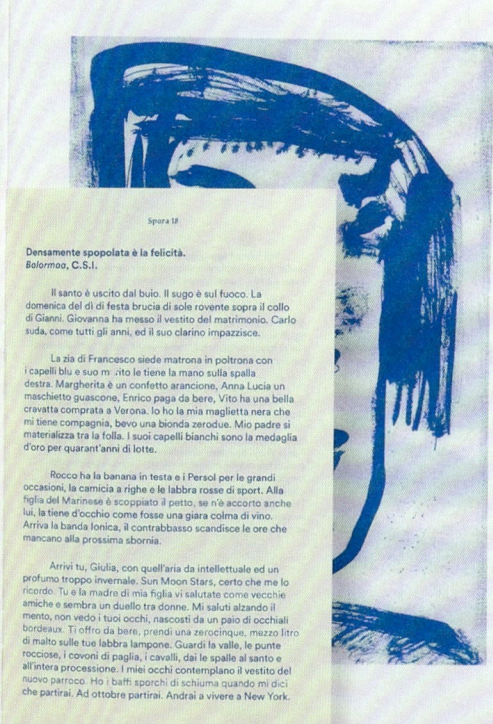

8.4 + 8.5

Sudario is a photographic fanzine curated by The View From Lucania. Its aim is to describe the south of Italy absorbing its most striking and axiomatic features revealing its shadows, stains, folds and moods. *Sudario* is printed in two color with a Risograph Rp3505 and it's assembled manually in a limited number edition of 60 copies.

Studio: Atto

Website: www.atto.si

Client: The View form Lucania

Index compiled by to Indexing Specialists (UK) Ltd